# Transformational Boards

Byron L. Tweeten
Growth Design Corporation

# Transformational Boards

## A Practical Guide to Engaging Your Board and Embracing Change

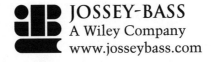

JOSSEY-BASS
A Wiley Company
www.josseybass.com

Published by

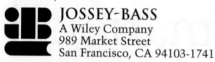 **JOSSEY-BASS**
A Wiley Company
989 Market Street
San Francisco, CA 94103-1741

www.josseybass.com

Copyright © 2002 by Byron L. Tweeten.

Jossey-Bass is a registered trademark of John Wiley & Sons, Inc.

Jossey-Bass books and products are available through most bookstores. To contact Jossey-Bass directly, call (888) 378–2537, fax to (800) 605–2665, or visit our website at www.josseybass.com.

Substantial discounts on bulk quantities of Jossey-Bass books are available to corporations, professional associations, and other organizations. For details and discount information, contact the special sales department at Jossey-Bass.

We at Jossey-Bass strive to use the most environmentally sensitive paper stocks available to us. Our publications are printed on acid-free recycled stock whenever possible, and our paper always meets or exceeds minimum GPO and EPA requirements.

The quotation from K. T. Greenfeld's article "A New Way of Giving" in Chapter Six is © 2000 by Time Inc. Reprinted by permission.

The quotation from George Starcher's article "Socially Responsible Enterprise Restructuring" in Chapter Six is used by permission of George Starcher.

**Library of Congress Cataloging-in-Publication Data**
Tweeten, Byron L., date-
    Transformational boards: a practical guide to engaging your board and embracing change / Byron L. Tweeten.—1st ed.
        p. cm.—(The Jossey-Bass nonprofit and public management series)
    Includes bibliographical references and index.
    ISBN 0-7879-5913-8 (alk. paper)
    1. Nonprofit organizations—Management. 2. Organizational change—Management. 3. Organizational effectiveness. I. Title. II. Series.
HD62.6 .T84 2002
658.4'063—dc21                                          2001006210

FIRST EDITION
*HB Printing*   10 9 8 7 6 5 4 3 2 1

The Jossey-Bass

Nonprofit and Public Management Series

*To my important mentors—*
*clients, colleagues, and family,*
*the best being my parents,*
*Delores and Lehman.*

# Contents

# Preface

At the core of *Transformational Boards* is the premise that nonprofit boards across the country need to seriously rethink their roles in this new century. This book is organized as a quick and user-friendly road map for executive leaders—both board members and top managers—as they reflect on their roles and duties together.

We, at Growth Design Corporation, acknowledge that there has been an enormous amount of literature published over the past decade on the roles of board members. Much of this information is excellent. However, our focus in this book goes beyond being a good board member. We discuss how boards today need to become much more fully engaged as they face the intense forces of change that are affecting, or will very soon affect, most nonprofit organizations. This book emerges from a deep desire to be helpful to boards as they redefine their roles during this challenging transformation process and plan for the future.

*Transformational Boards* focuses on an engagement model for board leadership. Our experience has shown us that through the application of this model, boards can best lead their organizations through times of change. Boards and CEOs can work closely together to set responsibilities, goals, and objectives for the organization. The board is also actively involved in setting policy, planning, communicating with constituents, and evaluating the board and CEO.

Each chapter identifies issues, cites relevant research, presents practical how-to examples and advice, and includes study questions to stimulate thinking and discussion. The chapters cover key issues that we know fully engaged boards must address in order to provide optimal leadership for organizations. In Chapter One, we look at ways to effectively recruit both board members and senior management. We then, in Chapter Two, examine the board's need to prepare for a high level of performance as their organizations face significant change. In Chapter Three, we cover how engaged boards must be actively involved in policy formation and review.

Chapter Four focuses on the importance of continuous thinking and planning as boards lead their organizations through change. Chapter Five discusses techniques for building on relationships to position and market an organization. In addition, we take a comprehensive look at a range of resource solutions in Chapter Six, including philanthropy, process redesign, enterprise development, collaboration, and stewardship. The aim is to develop revenues for organizations that can no longer depend on one resource to support their mission. In Chapter Seven, we emphasize the need for performance evaluation in order to keep board members and management on track toward reaching their objectives.

*Transformational Boards* is organized so that chapters can be read either consecutively or in a different order, depending on the specific concerns and interests of the reader; each chapter can be read and understood independently of the others. For some board members or senior managers, it may be helpful to read the book or specific chapters just prior to attending a board meeting. To promote dialogue, perhaps at a retreat or workshop, all participants might be asked to read the book and then discuss its implications for their organization. A checklist for engaged board members is included in the Appendix to help boards determine if they are on track for these dynamic times.

This book will be helpful to new nonprofit board members, as well as to longtime board members in need of a fresh focus and new energy. It will also be helpful to CEOs and other key managers in organizations as they work with their boards to face times of great change. We hope that nonprofit leaders who have already made a commitment to community service will now have an opportunity to maximize their contributions to the organizations and communities they serve. In the process, we think that both board members and executives can look forward to a more productive and satisfying relationship with their colleagues.

This book is the result of a collaborative effort at Growth Design Corporation—a consulting and professional services firm that offers resource solutions, integrated with Best Business Practice, to nonprofit organizations. Our team of senior professionals has worked extensively in the United States and Europe with clients such as colleges and universities; religious organizations; health, social service, and cultural organizations; and community-based service and development groups and associations. Our perspective into board development is the result of this breadth of experience. We hope that with this book we can extend the knowledge and experience we have gained with our clients to a wider audience of nonprofit organization board members and senior managers.

*Naples, Florida*                                        Byron L. Tweeten
*January 2002*

# Acknowledgments

The genesis of this book can be traced to several important sources. The first is the accumulated learning and experiences I have had working with hundreds of boards and CEOs of nonprofit organizations since 1969. My task has been to assist organizations, through their leaders, to become positioned for change and growth and to achieve their goals and objectives. Integrating the best of business practices with resource solutions is a primary ingredient in achieving the objectives or visions defined by boards and their senior management.

The key to developing and sustaining these essential business and resource elements for organizational growth resides with the quality, depth, and commitment of an organization's leadership—its board and senior management. In my experience, the most successful nonprofit organizations have developed a partnership between the board and senior management that engages leadership more strongly in a relationship that ensures a smooth transformation and sufficient resources during a time of change.

A second source for this book comes from my interaction with my colleagues at Growth Design Corporation on the topic of leadership development and its impact on policy and management, as well as on strategic thinking and planning. Our experience continues to evolve as we discuss the case studies on leadership development in and around our client base. These discussions continue to refine our thinking about the critical role of leadership as an asset to be managed and leveraged by organizations as they undertake transformational strategies to position themselves for growth.

Finally, the network of relationships represented by our client base in the United States and in other countries crosses over more and more into other nonprofit organizations, for-profit corporations, and other associations and service institutions that no longer fit a strict nonprofit definition. Rather, they are mission-focused entities that have chosen to organize in a variety of ways in support of a defined mission and strategic goal. The role of effective leadership within these organizations is critical to their decision making and to the accomplishment of their missions. This book, then, is intended to make our experiences and knowledge related to nonprofit boards accessible to other organizations facing similar issues and challenges in their own leadership strategies.

I would like to acknowledge my colleagues at Growth Design Corporation for their contributions to the book:

Carol Becker, senior consultant, for her strategic thinking around the subject of leadership, especially as it relates to team building

Kay Edwards, senior research consultant, for her contribution to the discussion of how target marketing and positioning relate to leadership and policy development

Gary Hubbell, senior consultant, for his development of content and background literature regarding various board leadership models and testing them with client boards

Ron Laughter, senior strategist, for his critical review and case development

David Lichter, senior consultant, for the content he provided and his strategic thinking related to board and CEO assessments, board and CEO recruitment, and relationships

Bill Luetscher, senior consultant, for his critical review and writing assistance

Wendy Lundquist, senior financial officer, for managing critical resources in the development of the knowledge in this manuscript

Jim Raffel, senior consultant, for his critical review and contributions to case development

Michelle Schultz and Michelle Bauer, for their research, project management, and sourcing assistance

And finally, I would like to thank Susan Montgomery, president of Chestnut Communications, Inc., for her significant contributions in strategic thinking and in the writing and editing of the complete manuscript.

# The Author

*Byron L. Tweeten*, chairman and CEO of Growth Design Corporation, has provided consulting services to some of the most significant and largest nonprofit organizations in the world. Tweeten began his career in 1969 by organizing a neighborhood-based nonprofit foundation whose mission was—and remains—to serve urban children, youth, and their families.

He organized Growth Design Corporation in 1981 after serving as a senior development officer in a private college. The firm is known for innovative thinking in business practices integrated with resource solutions, for assembling high-quality teams for service delivery, and for its commitment to building and maintaining strong relationships with its clients.

A cum laude graduate of Wartburg College, Mr. Tweeten holds an advanced degree in administrative leadership from the University of Wisconsin-Milwaukee. He has also been honored by his clients in various ways. For example, he received an honorary LLD degree from Concordia College in Nebraska for his sustained professional and personal commitment to mission-based organizations and for innovative services related to the development of the Concordia University System—a campus system that includes ten college and university campuses throughout the United States.

More recently, Tweeten's domestic clients have asked him to develop the ability to assist them as they connect their missions to partnerships throughout the world. He has taken a learning-and-listening approach, observing and building key relationships with leaders of vision and courage in nongovernmental organizations throughout Europe, Asia, the Middle East, and Africa. This new knowledge is now being applied in client situations in the United States and in selected countries.

Tweeten resides in Naples, Florida, and commutes to client settings throughout the world.

# About Growth Design Corporation

Growth Design serves mission-driven organizations that promote the common good in communities throughout the world. Its clients include every level of educational institution, a variety of health and long-term care organizations, fraternal organizations and associations, churches, religious denominations, human services organizations, and community development initiatives.

Growth Design's mission is to ensure the strength and growth of mission-driven organizations. Since 1981, Growth Design has assembled, integrated, and supported high-quality resource and organizational development teams for hundreds of nonprofit organizations and nongovernmental agencies.

Growth Design consulting teams are made up of seasoned professionals experienced in resource solutions integrated with business practices. Tailored service teams are developed to work with clients based on an organization's unique needs and culture. Additionally, many of the company's senior consultants are based throughout the nation, allowing the firm to partner with clients both nationally and internationally.

Growth Design's client leaders (boards and CEOs) cite innovation, relationship management, and high-quality service as signature characteristics of the firm's work. Frequent quality checks within a diverse patronage reflect the highest praise.

Growth Design's service delivery is based on a partnership with each client leader, built on trust and integrity. In this way, Growth Design is able to work with these leaders to design the template for their organization's mission and objectives.

Growth Design's client service center is located in Milwaukee, Wisconsin, with consultant offices located nationwide. They can be reached by calling (414) 224-0586 or by visiting their Web site: www.growthdesign.com.

# Transformational Boards

# Introduction: Nonprofit Boards Face Change

Dynamic, visionary boards are absolutely critical to the future of nonprofit, service-delivery organizations and, in fact, to the health of our society as a whole. Nonprofit organizations provide important solutions for our society, attacking day-to-day problems in the realms of learning, health care, family, community, religion, business, government, the environment, the arts, and more. The board decisions that guide these organizations have an enormous impact on individual members of communities, as well as on nonprofits themselves.

Boards in the twenty-first century are facing inevitable changes as a result of dramatic and continuing societal changes. These changes include the way people learn, the way they view authority, philanthropy, and nonprofit organizations, and the way they live, work, and play with emphasis on independence, self-development, flexibility, rapidly moving technology, and the family unit.

Transformational boards are fully engaged leaders performing their roles and responsibilities as nonprofit organizations transition from one area to another based on environmental factors. Rapid changes causing transformational activity are placing boards, as overseers of the public trust and as the ultimate policymakers, in the transformational process, demanding a deeper involvement, more intense and more rapid as the pace of change continues to increase.

These changes are taking place both globally and at the community level and are driven by social trends, economic forces, and technological innovation. Board members face all of these changes as they fulfill their multiple roles in setting policy, planning, developing resources, and overseeing delicate organizational transitions into the future.

The resource and organizational pressures generated by all these changes are perhaps greater than at any other time. Planning has become more difficult. Opportunities abound but require human and financial resources to develop and pursue them. Organizational alliances are both forming and dissolving. Leaders require nimble, responsive organizations. Constituents' desires and expectations change rapidly with the environment. For all these reasons, effective communication on all fronts is needed now more than ever.

Rosabeth Moss Kanter emphasizes this inevitability of change in an article in *Ivey Business Journal:*

> Organizational change has become a way of life as a result of three forces: globalization, information technology, and industry consolidation. In today's world, all organizations, from the Fortune 500 to the local nonprofit agency, need greater reach. They need to be in more places, to be more aware of regional and cultural differences, and to integrate into coherent strategies the work occurring in different markets and communities. [Kanter, 2000, p. 32]

Against this turbulent and dynamic backdrop, forward-looking nonprofit leaders are looking for help. The issue may be a need to generate more philanthropic support, or to identify and launch a new business venture, or to redesign the way decisions are reached and implemented, or to chart a new course for the organization— or to do all of this and more. In *Transformational Boards*, our goal is to provide guidance in this process of dramatic change. In particular, we are proposing that boards adopt an engagement model for board leadership that will keep them deeply involved in the crucial process of responding successfully to the changes they are confronting.

## Learning from Business

Readers will notice that much of the terminology and some examples used throughout the book are business-oriented. This is not an accident. We firmly believe that nonprofit boards have much to learn from their corporate counterparts, particularly as they face the pressures and demands of a changing environment. This is not to say that business cannot learn from nonprofits. The engagement model of board leadership is very much in line with many successful business governance models. The major and very crucial difference between nonprofit boards and corporate boards is that nonprofit boards are for the most part protected from taxation. This difference must be preserved, but nonprofit boards need to acknowledge that in many cases business practices can help their organizations advance their missions. As you progress through the book, you will see many examples of how nonprofit boards can benefit immensely by adopting business approaches to achieving their governance objectives.

## Facing and Embracing Change

*Transformational Boards* is about becoming an engaged, effective board member in a changing organization. An organization usually decides to change for one of four reasons: (1) marketplace trends, (2) a weak or obsolete business model, (3) a need for increased resources in order to meet the organization's mission, or (4) to stay ahead of competition. Sometimes a combination of these factors launches an organization down the path of change. In any case, organizations facing any of these situations are almost inevitably poised to begin a transformation process, or they may already be in the midst of one.

Here are some key questions leaders can ask about their organizations as they determine where they are in the process of change:

Are significant changes occurring in the organization's target-market constituent group that make its purpose, delivery systems, or business model obsolete?

Has there been a fundamental shift in the way the organization does business because of rapid change? (For instance, is the organization changing from being product-driven to being customer-focused?)

Are certain departments or divisions in the organization faltering because of an inability to respond to environmental shifts?

Has the organization created an alliance with a partner institution that has brought together two different cultures, requiring significant change in each other's modus operandi?

Is the life expectancy of the organization as it exists now less than two years, demanding a radical overhaul of the entire organization in order to survive?

Each of these situations requires a "crossing over"—a transformation—from one way of being to another. Transformation is an all-encompassing process and requires a fully engaged leadership, a change strategy, a process design or redesign, and project management that extends to all the human, organizational, and financial dynamics that come into play. Leaders on all levels need to partner with their constituents to identify issues and opportunities, develop solutions, and establish future goals. Board members need to understand what is expected of them as they participate in this transformation process. Many boards today, in partnership with their CEOs, have approved powerful missions and visions for the future and have identified ambitious goals but have not established a well-thought-out process of transformation in order to reach those goals.

## Addressing Problems

The problems and dilemmas leaders of nonprofit organizations face today stem from major organizational issues related to change and to the development of resources. These issues interact and must be addressed by boards in an integrated way if their organizations are to survive. Over the last decade, many boards have elected to close their organization's doors or, in some cases, to move to a for-profit status. Some boards have made wise but difficult decisions to close doors; for other boards, their organization's survival is crucial for the communities they serve. Nonprofit organizations are tax-exempt because they provide a service deemed important for the good of the community. However, some organizations either outlive their usefulness or solve the problems that drove the development of the organization in the first place. Organizations that are absolutely critical to the future of the community and to global well-being should be operating at peak performance to prepare for the ever-larger challenges of the future.

### Acquisitions and Mergers

The organizations with foresight and vision—the ones that recognize emerging trends—are the organizations that will operate successfully in the future. Remembering or looking at the past from the perspective of what's happening now also provides valuable lessons for the future operation of boards. We can look at many examples from a range of nonprofit arenas, including health care, social service, education, and religion that dramatically underscore this point. For instance, the American Hospital Association (Wright, 1997) reported in 1997 that 756 hospitals closed between 1980 and 1995. The same article states, "Facilities are frequently opting to consolidate or merge (which may or may not result in closures), form or join health networks, or shut down a portion of operations" (p. 22).

Mergers and acquisitions formerly existed only in the for-profit arena, and the government was not overly concerned about unrelated business income and property tax for nonprofits. Today, nonprofits all over the country are involved in mergers and acquisitions due to changes in customer demands, lack of resources, competitive and economic pressures, and the fact that some organizations have been run very successfully with good business models and cash reserves. This is likely to continue in all sectors of nonprofits; therefore, boards will frequently be asked to think about partnerships, collaborations, mergers, and acquisitions. The tax issue will also continue to emerge as nonprofit margins increase and diversification of services occurs.

Not so long ago, hospitals and nursing homes were exclusively nonprofits, and their leaders were usually from church or civic backgrounds. Health care organizations that anticipated the transformation that has been taking place in the health care industry have been better able to survive in today's dynamic health care climate. Profitable hospitals throughout the country today have significant margins that are often due to mergers, acquisitions, or restructuring of ownership.

Social service agencies—many of which were originally launched by private interests, community interests, and philanthropy—eventually came to be primarily dependent on government funding. However, as government funding becomes more and more restricted or shifts of policy or priorities occur, resource options are changing. And this is happening while the traditional missions of feeding the hungry, clothing the poor, and providing shelter for people in need are intensifying. Philanthropy and other key funding sources are again providing a substantial percentage of revenue for these agencies. Many social service boards need to decide whether or not to continue providing the same services and then determine how to fund those services.

### Changes in Educational and Religious Organizations

Visionary institutions of higher education determined more than a decade ago that they could not rest on the glory of their insular campuses of the past. If many had not embraced the concepts of lifelong learning and long-distance learning, they would have not survived. Like health care, higher education is moving toward non-site delivery systems, and the entire realm of education must address the following issues: technology and costs are driving dramatic changes; reengineering or business process redesign is under way; the composition of student populations is changing. Higher education boards must engage in intense discussions about policies as they relate to all of these issues.

Religious organizations have been reeling from dramatic transformation for quite some time. Due to the "softening" of mainline denominations, chaos is emerging in many religious organizations. Downsizing, reorganization, consolidation, and retrenchment are all current agendas at the Christian denomination level. Key trends continue to be a localization of resources and the emergence of megamovements, sects, and diverse theologies that are outside the traditional structure of the Christian church. Religious board agendas are pointing to the need for transformation within their organizations while building their faith communities so constituents can continue to worship, study, and serve.

Nonprofit boards need to anticipate and plan for major shifts in funding sources and for increased competition for philanthropic dollars. The *Nonprofit Almanac* states:

> Competition between non-profit and for-profit organizations at the state level in contracting for a variety of services with the federal government will accelerate in the areas of health services, job training, family services, and residential care. At the same time, as government funding declines or shifts, competition among non-profits for private contributions will accelerate. . . . Accelerating competition for contributions among independent sector organizations may lead non-profits to form coalitions at the local level, to merge, and in some cases, to close. As organizations compete for private contributions and government funds, accountability and performance will become increasingly important. [Hodgkinson and Weitzman, 1996, p. 17]

## Addressing New Agenda Issues

As they work to fulfill their duties as representatives of the public trust and establish agendas that address key transformation and resource development issues, many boards today find themselves facing the following issues:

- Understanding what rapid changes in their constituent environments mean to their nonprofit organizations, particularly where public policy is affected
- Responding to rapid changes in technologies and delivery systems—changes that may have a dramatic impact on the balance of control between the organization and the customer
- Recognizing the importance of emerging boundaryless environments in organizations that now have regional, national, and global opportunities for alliances and service
- Understanding that the changing nature of relationships affects every aspect of an organization's operation and mission
- Focusing on a consumer-oriented marketplace
- Developing a continuous process to review and quickly adjust corporate direction, mission, and strategy based on group and community values and beliefs as environmental change occurs
- Understanding process redesign for efficiencies, resource reallocation, and systems development
- Understanding the transformation process, including planning, demonstration, abandonment (endings), and full acceptance and renewal
- Responding to a market's inability to pay for the increasingly sophisticated services that nonprofits are capable of delivering
- Understanding financial modeling and the mix of capitalization potential, including existing service revenues, new enterprise, philanthropy, investment management of reserves, process redesign, and strategic alliances
- Understanding the dynamics of pluralistic, multicultural, and mixed-gender boards and responding to the divergent values and experiences of those boards
- Designing programs for staff orientation and training in the multifaceted, rapidly changing area of resource development

Boards need to address these issues. They can no longer waste precious meeting time on irrelevant or insignificant agenda items that have no direct impact on their missions. In order to make critical decisions for the future, board members and their supporting management teams must understand the environment, the organization's current capabilities and position, the changes necessary, and the process of transformation. This understanding is not a one-time realization but should be addressed each time a board meets.

## Confronting Threats to Board Effectiveness

In addition to facing these crucial issues, individual boards may also find themselves facing some troubling trends among individual board members—trends that are inhibiting the growth and development of these organizations. In the past, some boards with weak members may have been able to operate inefficiently and still get by, but this will not be possible as organizations face the transformation process that is inevitable if they are to be successful in this new century. Boards can no longer afford to be dysfunctional.

As we work with boards, we often observe members arriving and opening a sealed envelope that had been mailed to them by the CEO. These board members are obviously not prepared for the meeting and probably did not come with the kinds of well-considered questions, observations, and concerns necessary for substantive input regarding difficult issues affecting the organization.

We have also observed agendas that do not deal with important, timely issues but with historical financial reports and reports about past program activity. There is a dangerous tendency for many boards to be so emotionally attached to their history that they overvalue the past and are reluctant to embrace necessary change. The leaders of these boards may engage the group in very little discussion about policies, plans, resource strategies, and leadership issues related to direction, environment, and self-evaluation—all issues that must be addressed for change to take place. The pace of change is so rapid that if boards pause when they should be deciding and acting, they could be contributing to the demise of the very mission they were recruited to serve.

The following key trends need to be recognized and addressed by nonprofit boards facing the challenges of transformation:

- Limited availability of board members, resulting in inadequate participation in board activities
- Lack of preparation of board members, resulting in less productive board meetings
- Lack of recruitment strategies, resulting in boards that are unable to attract and keep effective board members
- Board members who are on too many boards, thus limiting their participation on any one board
- Lack of continuity among board membership because of departing board members
- Boards that are unwieldy and difficult to support because they are too large
- Boards that are ineffective because they don't understand the environment in which they are operating
- Board members who do not understand their roles as fully engaged board members
- Board members and CEOs who fail to form partnerships, resulting in policies and agendas that don't carry the organization forward

When the CEO sets policy and agendas without board involvement, the board is often left with little or no impact, and agendas may result that don't target real issues or lead to solutions for the organization's future.

## Using the Engagement Model in Times of Change

Boards of organizations facing major change will be most effective if they are fully engaged in the processes of preparations, policy review, planning, resource development, public relations, and positioning in the marketplace. The engagement model of board leadership proposes that boards and senior management work closely together to set agendas, policies, responsibilities, and objectives for their organizations.

In today's world, the role of the nonprofit board is complex. Busy CEOs, in partnership with boards, often have trouble knowing where to begin when it comes to dealing with the support and management needed to move boards to function properly. Although nonprofit organizations have changed in many arenas, models for board governance have only recently started to change. Many theorists and practitioners still propose that the board's role is to simply be a policymaking body and that the organization's CEO should represent the board and manage day-to-day operations. Many organizations still operate in this fashion, and this may work for some boards; however, many visionary boards that are either preparing for or are in the midst of significant change have discovered that an engagement model for board leadership is more effective.

The chart shown in Table I.1 presents a continuum of board involvement from the popular policy-centered model to the operational model in which the board actively participates in both program planning and implementation.

The engagement model, which falls toward the center of the continuum shown, provides guidelines for a board that is actively involved in seven key areas of organizational leadership:

1. *Leadership Recruitment:* An engaged board is integrally involved in CEO recruitment and in the recruitment of its own board members. Too many times in the past, board members have relegated these responsibilities to small committees or outside consultants. Although consultants can be invaluable during the recruitment process, board members still need to be actively involved. This involvement will result in a more cohesive and productive partnership between board members and newly recruited leaders. Board members are also engaged in determining how the board will function, what its

**Table I.1. Three Models of Board Leadership**

| Governance Elements | Policy-Centered Model | Engagement Model | Operational Model |
|---|---|---|---|
| Leadership Recruitment | • The board establishes lists of acceptable and unacceptable actions for the board, CEO, and staff. | • The board and the CEO define a format for role and meeting preparations, orientation, and communication strategies and tools. | • The board chair or executive committee oversees the CEO and determines board operations. |
| Preparation for High Performance | • Prescriptive action steps are taken for all organizations. | • Board members study market trends; observe organizational service and programs; study current literature; attend selected forums, seminars, and conferences; and review material prepared by the CEO before meetings. | • Meetings are informal and depend on the chair's working style and time availability. |
| Policy Review and Formation | • There is little staff or CEO input into policy formation and little or no committee structure within the board. | • Board decisions on policy are based on a continuous review format, in partnership with the CEO and senior staff. | • The board reacts to policies set by the CEO and staff. |
| Continuous Thinking and Planning | • Decisions are based primarily on program or service audiences and budgets. | • The board, CEO, and senior management are engaged in a continuous review of planning-process design, strategic thinking, and the approval of values, mission, and vision. | • Members are actively involved in program planning, implementation, and oversight, often in place of paid staff. |

| | | |
|---|---|---|
| Positioning and Public Relations | • The board dictates policy related to research and reviews positioning for organizational policy formation; publics are broadly defined as the general public ownership (trust). | • "Publics" are defined as specific, targeted constituent groups. The board actively participates in a review of constituent research for policy formation and planning, at times engaging in actively listening to peers and the CEO for feedback. | • Listening is often anecdotal, based on a close relationship to customer and program implementation, typically with a short-term view. |
| Financial Resource Solutions | • The board sets policy for resources, with no expectation for involvement, and is not receptive to new ideas for resource solutions. | • The board is involved in policymaking, strategic thinking, and actively partnering with the CEO, senior management, and other volunteers involved in implementation. Members are philanthropic regarding time, talent, and financial resources. | • Giving by board members is uneven. Often there is reliance on "emergency" funding from specific board members. The board is limited in resource solutions and strategies. |
| Performance Evaluation | • The board is active in CEO performance evaluation.<br>• The board and CEO work together to set responsibility, goals, and objectives for both the board and the CEO. | • Board members regularly self-assess their individual and performance groups and are responsible for the evaluation of the CEO, based on performance indicators. | • Committees oversee staff and projects; evaluation is informal or nonexistent. |

agendas will be, where they will meet and when, and how committees will be structured.

2. *Preparation for High Performance:* The engagement model calls for board meetings that are well organized and productive and that move the organization forward. This means that board members must actively prepare for meetings before they begin. They must come to meetings fully informed and ready to make sound decisions on all agenda items. They are also engaged in determining how the board will function, operate, and meet, as well as in what the committee structure will be.

3. *Policy Review and Formation:* Policy review is a fluid process for an engaged board in times of great change. Boards and CEOs need to work together to review and alter policies, if necessary, to reflect changes in the organization's mission, market, and environment.

4. *Continuous Thinking and Planning:* Although in the past many boards left planning to their CEOs, planning in the engagement model is continuous and takes place in partnership with senior management. Only through this continuous, active approach to planning can boards be assured that they are responding to their rapidly changing environments.

5. *Positioning and Public Relations:* Engaged boards need to actively participate in constituent prioritization and research so they are always in touch with their changing markets.

6. *Financial Resource Solutions:* Evaluating, exploring, and developing an appropriate combination of resource solutions may be the most crucial area demanding board involvement. Nonprofit organizations today can no longer rely on one or two static sources of revenue. Every avenue for developing funds must be explored, including philanthropy, process redesign, enterprising, collaboration, and stewardship.

7. *Performance Evaluation:* Board members and senior management need to be performing at the highest levels when change

is taking place. It is up to the board to regularly evaluate both itself and its management leaders to ensure that objectives are being met and planning is on track. Boards that don't evaluate may find themselves floundering and wonder why. Without productive leaders moving in the same direction, an organization is going nowhere.

Traditionally, the larger and more sophisticated the organization, the more likely its governance model is to move toward the left of the continuum; governance of smaller and lower-budget organizations is more likely to move toward the right. However, there is so much at stake during a time of great change that many nonprofit boards, including those at either end of the continuum—policy-centered boards and operational boards—need to move toward the engagement model in the center.

There are many well-known and successful policy-centered models, such as the Carver model (see Carver and Carver, 1996a). And there are other approaches to board functioning. However, many models that worked well in the past will not work nearly as effectively during a time of organizational transformation. The engagement model responds to the needs of a dynamic organization in the midst of transformation.

In *Your Roles and Responsibilities as a Board Member* (Carver and Carver, 1996b), the importance of a fully involved board, even in the context of the Policy Governance model, is emphasized in the following quote:

> Board members can be successful strategic leaders if they nurture their sense of group responsibility. All members must participate in the discipline and productivity of the group. All members must be willing to challenge and urge each other on to big dreams, lucid values, and fidelity to their trusteeship. [p. 1]

A new partnership needs to emerge between board members and management that suggests a larger role for board leaders. This role, at times, moves beyond policy into planning and relates to understanding the marketplace and to listening and communicating on behalf of the organization. Board members must operate as a group, commit at the highest levels, and act as strategic partners with their CEOs, fulfilling essential roles related to planning, public relations, and resource development.

The chapters that follow focus on the key elements in Growth Design Corporation's approach to board leadership, as reflected in the engagement model. The chapters are designed to clarify the more complex roles required of nonprofit board members today and describe how organizations can use leadership to change, transform, and develop significant resources, resulting in a strengthening of organizational missions that better serve the community.

*Chapter One*

# Leadership Recruitment

The entrepreneurial nonprofit executive
understands that he or she can only control the
future, not the past, and that it is when upcoming
realities are in their formative stage that they can
be shaped most easily.

*Thomas McLaughlin*

In this chapter, board members will learn how their full involvement in the recruitment process—of both senior management and their board colleagues—is crucial in order to take organizations successfully through times of great change.

George was recently recruited to be the president of a growing university after the previous president had left unexpectedly for another position. At the same time, the university's board of directors was involved in redefining its mission, evaluating its market, and establishing strategic plans for an inevitable major organizational transformation. However, these agenda items were put on hold in order to quickly fill the vacated president's position. George's background and experience as president of a smaller, similar university reflected those of his predecessor, who was very successful from the board's perspective. However, after George was hired a financial crisis emerged, and the board determined that the university needed to make major changes in its market and consider embracing new technologies in delivering education. George did not have experience with the new market of students and was accustomed to traditional

17

ways of providing education. He found himself frustrated and felt at a loss as to how to deal with these changes. The board was also frustrated at George's inability to meet its new expectations and eventually asked him to resign. The board then appointed an interim president—a current board member who understood the new directions the board needed to take. Meanwhile, a presidential search was launched that focused on the organization's current and future leadership needs.

In a time of change, strong board and CEO leadership is crucial to steer an organization through the inevitable upheavals it will encounter. Board members adhering to the engagement model of board leadership understand this and are involved in the crucial recruitment process. People are the most important part of the transformation process. Without the support of key leaders, the organization cannot be changed. An organization's leaders need to have the ability to guide employees through the process—to help them see the value in carrying out the changes that must take place.

Especially important to the process of carrying out change is leadership that can motivate and inspire an organization to move energetically in the targeted direction. Only strong leaders who understand this necessity can engender a culture of empowering employees to move forward and keep needed change on track. Without this culture, organizationwide change will not be successful.

John Kotter says in his book, *Leading Change* (1996), "Only leadership can blast through the many sources of corporate inertia. Only leadership can motivate the actions needed to alter behavior in any significant way. Only leadership can get change to stick by anchoring it in the very culture of an organization" (p. 30).

## Recruiting Board Members

As boards consider the process of recruiting board members, it may be valuable to examine the motivations people have for joining boards, especially the motivations for joining their particular board. Board members should ask themselves, "Why did I join this board?

What will motivate others to join?" The answers to these questions may be far-reaching and multifaceted. In all likelihood, many factors combine to convince a person to join a board of directors, including social prestige, opportunity for impact, personal or business connections to the board's mission, other special interests, or funding sources; others include the person's ethnicity, gender, age, or geography.

It is important before beginning the recruiting process to define those factors for a particular organization. Understanding motivation will help immensely in identifying, attracting, and keeping new board members. It will also help to realize that a well-balanced board undoubtedly has members who have joined for a variety of reasons. If everyone joined a board for the same reason, it would be a boring board—and probably not a very effective one.

The kind of board members an organization needs during major change may be very different from the kind needed in the past. Consequently, it is important for the board to identify the characteristics new members need. One key goal is to recruit board members who understand and embrace the need for change.

The ideal situation calls for recruiting board members who already have an understanding and appreciation of the organization. Nothing is more disconcerting to a prospective board member than receiving a phone call out of the blue with a request to join the board of an organization the prospect knows little or nothing about. A better approach is to have a board development committee identify prospective board members and encourage their involvement in the organization's activities.

For instance, these prospective members could be on ad hoc action teams or advisory councils. This gives the prospect an opportunity to understand the work and challenges of the organization and the board a chance to get to know the prospective board member, seeing firsthand the person's capabilities and commitment to the group. This approach isn't always possible, but the prospective board member should always have the opportunity to learn about the organization before making a decision to join the board.

In addition, the board's expectations for board members should be made very clear to the prospect in advance. For instance, what will the demands of the transformation process mean to board members? What are attendance expectations? What level of involvement is anticipated? If board members are expected to participate in philanthropy, either as donors or as fundraisers (or both), this needs to be clarified before the relationship begins. With nonprofit boards, members are typically expected to participate in philanthropy as a resource solution. Too many times these expectations are not discussed up-front, and serious issues emerge after the member has joined. However, looking at wealth or the potential for giving as the only criteria for board member selection is rarely a good idea. Farsighted boards seek well-rounded board members who can contribute time, talents, and resources on many fronts as the organization moves forward.

Most effective boards thrive with representation from diverse backgrounds. They look for prospective leaders who are not already serving on numerous other community boards and who represent a range of an organization's constituencies. In many communities, certain people are on multiple boards. In a recent survey conducted by the National Center for Nonprofit Boards (2000, p. 32), 14.4 percent of respondents served on three boards, 7.4 percent served on four boards, and 4.6 percent served on five or more boards.

Busy business people serving on too many boards tend to be overly committed and unable to participate actively. In addition, they may not represent the diverse range of leaders an organization needs to move effectively through times of change. Organizations need to look carefully at their prospective board members' other involvements. It is essential to have board members who have the time and commitment for full participation, particularly during a challenging transformation process.

## Handling Transitions with Care

Board membership beginnings need to be well planned. If this does not happen, a new board member's initial board experience may be problematic and lead to premature resignation or an ineffective use of talent. Orienting a new member to the board of an organization involves a range of complex issues and challenges. Not only do new board members need to fully understand the mission and operation of the organization but they need to understand the dynamics of board and management relationships. These new leaders also need to find their own roles on the board. Just handing new board members a stack of reading material is rarely an effective way to bring them into the organization. Board member orientation needs to be well planned and engage new members immediately.

The board, in partnership with the CEO, should think through the orientation process with the goal of building a successful team. Involving a new board member in a committee is a good way to integrate the person into the organization. Assigning a current board member as a mentor to the new person may also be helpful.

The orientation of new board members should include the following:

- *Review of the board's operating procedures:* How does the board operate? What is its role in the organization's structure? What are its responsibilities, and how does it fulfill them? What is its meeting schedule?

- *Definition of expectations for each board member:* What level of participation is expected of each board member? How should board members prepare for meetings? How will communication take place among board members and between board members and the organization's management? What role is the board member expected to take in philanthropy?

- *Profiles of the other board members and their roles in the board's structure and operation:* Develop each board member's biography to be reviewed by other board members. Why was the board member selected—for expertise, representation, or "other"? What committees or task groups does the board member serve on? Who are the officers, and are there other roles that board members play? How long do they serve? When does their term end?

- A *thorough briefing on the CEO and the board's expectations of the CEO:* What is the CEO's biography? What is the history of the CEO with the organization—longevity? What is the contract agreement with the CEO? What is the CEO's compensation, including incentives and benefits? How is the CEO currently evaluated? What specific goals and plans has the CEO committed to over the next year, the next three years? How do board members and the CEO interact?

- A *thorough review of all policies, operational plans, and budgets:* The changes that should be reviewed with particular care during the transformation process are these: Is there a listing of all policies? What are the operational plans for the next six months, for next year? What is the status of the current budget, cash flow, investments, assets, liabilities? What are the policies under review at the next meeting?

- A *complete review of the board's planning process:* How does the board assess itself related to its role and responsibilities? How does it engage in the overall planning process of the organization? Does it review its mission, vision, and values on a regular basis? How does the CEO engage the organization in strategic thinking about the future and planning of operational activity? Are there evaluation mechanisms regarding plans to be implemented?

- A *review of the organization's resources:* What support is being used to fund the organization's operations, quality improvements, new ventures, and development of reserves? How will plans being implemented during the transformation process be financed?

- A *breakdown of the current target market and also of marketplaces being contemplated:* What is the profile of the current target market or market niches? What market share are we serving? What is our ability to increase market share? What pricing strategies are we employing in relationship to services or products? What new markets are possible? What is the profile of the markets? How are the new markets similar to or different from existing markets? How is the current market surveyed, and what is the satisfaction level of services and products?

- *A complete description of the organization's products and services:* This process should include some experience or contact with those services. For instance, a new board member of a higher education institution should have had the experience of sitting through a few classes and of talking with students and professors.

- *Results of recent evaluations of the organization, the board, and the CEO:* Usually these are confidential, and therefore certain policies may be in place regarding published reports. How does each board member receive these reports? What is the schedule for evaluations? What mechanisms and processes are used? What committees or task groups are involved? What is the current evaluation of the organization's programs, services, and products, of its accomplishment of plans and targeted goals, of the board and its role, and of the CEO and the stated expectations by the board?

- *Results of recent customer satisfaction surveys:* What is the opinion of constituents or customers regarding the program, service, or product they used? Did it meet their expectation? What improvements would they contemplate? How often do they use the program, service, or product? What would encourage them to use it more? Would they recommend it to peers? What new services, products, or programs would they encourage the organization to think about? Is it priced right? Are the channels of delivery appropriate? Is there a better way to access the program, service, or product?

All this information cannot be conveyed in one meeting. A thorough member orientation may take place over several months; many board members would like to have a much more extensive orientation than is typical. It is particularly important for board members to have a thorough understanding of an organization in order to lead it through a demanding process of major change.

Board membership endings need to be just as carefully considered as beginnings. Appropriate recognition and appreciation need to be expressed. If the board member leaving has been a valuable asset to the organization in the past, the same can be true for the future. Boards need to establish a way for former board members to maintain their relationship with the organization. They can be appointed to advisory groups or presidents' councils or be given some sort of emeritus status that involves a continuing involvement or relationship with the organization. All too often, valuable board members say good-bye and are never heard from again. This can be a great loss to the organization.

## Assuming an Active Role in Recruiting Peers

Many nonprofit boards take the process of choosing new board members too lightly; however, choosing effective board leaders is a crucial board responsibility and a key component of the engagement model of governance. Without proper attention to the board member selection process, new members may join the board without any relevant experience or cultivation and then exit quickly because they feel they don't belong. Just as the organization has a plan for its direction based on its mission, values, and strategies, there should be a plan for the board's recruitment and development of its own leadership. Many boards do not have a carefully considered plan for their own development—a plan that specifies what kind of leadership talent is needed in relationship to their organization's plans for the future and the transformation process.

Some boards have subgroups that regularly think about board recruitment. Sometimes called nominating committees or leadership development committees or teams, these groups think seriously about the criteria, characteristics, and talents needed to create a board that can provide strong leadership as the organization goes through major change. This needs to be an ongoing process because member criteria change as the organization changes. "Leadership development" is probably a more appropriate descriptor for this committee or team because this group may also assume a mentoring role for reviewing and evaluating a new board member's first year.

As the board recruiting process begins, it's also important to look at what an organization's bylaws say about board membership. When organizations are approved as tax-exempt, certain guidelines and restrictions are established for board members. Such issues as the size of boards, qualifications of board members, and length of board terms may be addressed in the bylaws. Sometimes policies haven't been reviewed for years and, as organizations go through transformation, the bylaws may need to be changed to accommodate the board's evolving needs. For instance, a board may decide that the term of board membership should change (perhaps made longer or shorter), based on the cycle of the organization and its plans and leadership needs during the transformation process.

## Establishing a Sound Recruitment Plan

An effective board recruitment plan should define the board's role in the organization and answer some of the following questions:

What kind of constituent representation do we need from the marketplace?

What kind of specific expertise do we need on this board?

How do we recruit board members who are team players and who can relate to others on the board?

How do we balance our need to have board members who believe in our organization's underlying values with the diversity that represents a broad constituency?

What kind of time and commitment expectations do we have for board members, including philanthropic expectations?

How do we determine if the prospective board member is respected by peers and constituents?

The answers to these questions should lead to the development of a board member profile that can be used during the member selection process.

## Recruiting the Right CEO

Having the right CEO who has the complete support of the board of directors is a cornerstone of the engagement model and is essential during times of change. The importance of recruiting the right CEO cannot be emphasized enough, especially in transforming environments.

The span of time that a CEO spends with an organization is relatively short. This is true across the nonprofit spectrum—at universities, hospitals, social service agencies, religious organizations, and cultural groups. According to an article in the *Chronicle of Higher Education* ("Diversity Increases . . . ," 2000) that reports on a recent survey of presidents, college presidents averaged 6.9 years on the job in 1998. That is only a little bit longer than an average planning cycle that typically ranges from three to five years.

This trend toward abbreviated CEO tenure puts strong pressure on boards of directors, both because of the frequency of a time-consuming recruiting process and the need to find the right person who will stay with the organization during a challenging period of transformation. The last thing a board needs is for the CEO to leave in the middle of an intense transformation process, yet this happens regularly, particularly when the wrong CEO is in place. Boards need to look closely at the organization and where it's going as they select appropriate leadership for the present and the future. The *Chronicle of Higher Education* (Basinger, 2001) notes, from the report titled "Presidential Succession and Transition: Beginning, Ending and Beginning Again," that "ample evidence suggests that many presidential transitions are untimely, poorly managed, personally dissatisfying and in some cases even demeaning for the primary players—the presidents themselves." The article "urges boards to comprehensively manage transitions—from the announcement of a president's departure through the search and into the early months of a new presidency and to help the president make key acquaintances both on and off the campus."

The short terms of so many CEOs result in a lack of leaders who have tenure and experience with the organization. Who in the organization brings the invaluable asset of an institutional memory that goes back more than a few years? If not the CEO, is it other staff members or board members (or consultants or constituents) who have the institutional memory? If you have short-term board members and a short-term CEO, you may have no organizational memory. When you consider the importance of developing relationships with a range of constituents and the time it takes to develop these relationships, the trend toward short terms (of both CEOs and board members) becomes a serious issue. This issue of having short-term CEOs is especially crucial when you consider that a major organizational transformation takes time—sometimes three to five years or more.

Why do CEOs leave their positions? A survey conducted in 1999 by CompassPoint Nonprofit Services revealed that of 137 nonprofit executive directors, only one-fourth of them would want another job as CEO of a nonprofit organization. When asked, "What would make you leave your job?," "burnout" and "seeking career growth" earned 26 percent of the responses (p. 2); however, following close behind with 22 percent of the responses was "problems with board relationships" (p. 2).

Despite the best intentions on the part of boards, this unhappy scenario repeats itself with disturbing regularity, particularly in non-profit organizations. In most cases, this happens because the board doesn't understand the importance of its role in hiring the CEO or misjudges the kinds of talents and characteristics needed to guide the organization through a period of transformation. This can happen if the board has not carefully analyzed its present and future position in the marketplace or doesn't have organizational plans to attach to the recruiting process.

## Balancing the CEO-Board Relationship

Recruiting a CEO demands a delicate balance between hiring someone strong enough to run the operation and yet interdependent enough to be responsive to the board's direction and policies. An essential tenet of the engagement model of board leadership is having a board and CEO that collaborate closely as they take their organization successfully through change.

In the engagement model, the CEO is still officially under the supervision of the board of directors; however, in the ideal situation the CEO and board work as partners supporting the mission of the organization. The CEO represents the board both within the organization and in the marketplace, but the right CEO assumes the position of leader of the transformation process. The board should expect the CEO to bring a vision of the future to the board and to provide leadership in the crucial consensus-building process among board members and managers.

It should be pointed out that in some nonprofit organizations, particularly the smaller ones, a wide variety of unique and workable relationships exist between boards and CEOs. Sometimes the CEO is actually a member of the board or functions as the president of the board as well as president of the organization. Although these kinds of relationships may not be the norm and are not generally recommended, they sometimes work well for individual organizations. However, even in these instances, boards and CEOs still need to strive for the appropriate balance in their relationships.

When a CEO has success and longevity, the board's role and the CEO's role can become blurred or reversed. In some cases, the CEO, however well meaning, may start to set policy and the board becomes an audience. Then if a crisis strikes, such as the unexpected resignation of the CEO, the diminished board may find itself incapable of managing the organization without a CEO or of mounting a solid recruitment program.

The relationship between the CEO and the board becomes critical during times when significant change is taking place. The best relationship is one where there is a partnership between the board and the CEO as they work together to implement change. The board and CEO may come to a consensus on the change that is needed, and the CEO then defines the transformation process for the board and the organization's managers. It is essential that the CEO has the complete confidence and support of the board of directors during the process of change. This can only happen if the right CEO is recruited and in place and if the board makes a commitment to support that CEO through the inevitable challenges and upheavals that characterize the transformation process.

## Choosing a CEO Who Is Poised for Change

Boards facing the intense challenges of change on many fronts need a CEO who has multiple talents and extensive experience. Specifically, boards may want their CEOS to have most or all of the characteristics discussed in the sections to follow.

### Be a Strong Leader Who Motivates Others

The person being considered for the CEO position needs to have a desire and ability to be a strong, motivational leader who can lead others in a direction they might not have initially considered. This person should be able to mobilize an organization's membership constituency through a unique ability to persuade and convince people of a new vision and direction. The leader should have the ability to clearly articulate and direct the mission and vision for the organization and be persistent in the face of obstacles. In particular, leaders during times of change should have high energy, empathy, and effective urgency, and they should not be afraid of risks that have been thoughtfully considered.

### Be Team-Oriented

A CEO should also be team-oriented and be able to partner with the board of directors in planning, developing policy, and seeking human and financial resource solutions. It is particularly important that the person be able to interpret organizational issues, trends, assumptions, and environmental changes; to lead teams; and assist in the planning of solutions. The CEO should be a strong consensus maker, a collaborator, and a communicator within an organization. The CEO should have a sense of vision and be able to articulate and appreciate a variety of perspectives. (Yes, we are asking a great deal of the CEO. You can see why finding the right CEO is a significant board challenge.)

### Have a Varied Background

A CEO with a varied and not necessarily traditional background can be a tremendous asset to an organization. A CEO who has had significant experience as a corporate board member or senior manager may have a special understanding of the unique qualities it takes to develop an effective board-CEO relationship. There are impressive examples of corporate business leaders who have taken over nonprofits and done an excellent job of bringing business experience to the organization; however, during the recruitment process, boards need to remember that nonprofits have a unique culture, and the CEO must be able to fit into that culture. Even though nonprofits increasingly recognize the need for stronger management, the first priority is still the mission, not the bottom line. It is the unique corporate CEO who can make the challenging transition to a nonprofit agency—a CEO who knows change and transformation and yet has an understanding of mission and process, as well as the ability to manage and direct.

### Relate Well to Others

A nonprofit organization is a relationship organization, and its market leaders need to be guided by their ability to empathize with and relate to people. Their excellent interpersonal relationship skills communicate to others their understanding of them and desire to be of service to them. They need to enjoy people, exhibiting a good degree of sociability and a comfort with people both one-on-one and in public settings. A modest degree of gregariousness indicates that a person can move within social settings with comfort, embodying the relationship nature of an organization. This person should be appropriately accommodating, not shrinking from the challenge to relate to the various constituencies represented in the organization's diverse publics—from the nursing home to the board room. Leaders also need an adequate degree of shrewdness or political savvy, including the ability to comprehend motives and agendas within any setting.

## Be a Creative Problem Solver

The leader of a transforming organization should be a creative problem solver and reliable in decision making. Given the strategic nature of nonprofit activity, this leader should possess the highest level of abstract reasoning. Leaders need to be bright, creative, open-minded, strategic, flexible thinkers who are not afraid of risk; they should feel the urgency in making decisions and yet possess sufficient thoroughness to make sound decisions. The CEO in a changing organization should be a creative change agent and risk taker because growth demands both change and risk. A CEO who doesn't have these characteristics isn't going to do very well in steering an organization through the choppy waves of change.

## Be in Touch with the Organization's Marketplace

The CEO should have a deep understanding of the organization's designated marketplace and a propensity to listen and interact within that marketplace. This means looking to the market of the future rather than the past. For instance, if a college or university is moving into a nontraditional market of working, older students, selecting a president who comes from the traditional college market orientation may be inappropriate. If a social service agency is neighborhood-based, it would seem wise to hire a leader who understands the needs and desires of that neighborhood or a similar neighborhood.

### Organize Time and Priorities Effectively

Nonprofit CEOs should be able to initiate, organize, prioritize, execute, and follow up on activities. Time and task management can often be delegated in leadership positions, yet the leader should have a degree of self-structure or self-discipline along with the ability to prioritize and accept tasks, as well as to monitor their implementation. While respecting existing policies, procedures, and processes, the leader should have the capability to set an innovative course and pilot the ship through inevitably turbulent waters.

It's not an easy task for boards to find prospective CEOs with these characteristics, but with a sound recruitment plan and a diligent approach, the boards' efforts will be well rewarded with highly effective leadership, particularly in times of change. However, it cannot be emphasized enough that even the ideal CEO, who may completely reflect the characteristics profiled here, will not be effective or successful without the support and involvement of the organization's board of directors.

## Knowing the Organization and Board

Boards ought to look carefully at where and how they recruit their CEOs. Boards need to be clear about what they believe in as a board, about their mission, and about how their organization is changing and transforming in relation to their marketplace. If the board doesn't understand itself and what its belief systems are and has not established a consensus around direction, it's unlikely that the recruitment process will result in the ideal candidate.

Rejection of offers is an increasing phenomenon in organizations. For instance, during an eighteen-month period, a prominent nonprofit organization in Minnesota offered its CEO position to three candidates who rejected the offer. Under pressure to hire a CEO, the organization then felt forced to choose an insider who had maintained the status quo well but had not effectively addressed emerging changes. In another instance, a church in Nebraska called six different pastors who all rejected the offer because it was obvious to these candidates that the church had not solved dysfunctional issues within the organization that carried through to the recruitment process.

The search for a CEO should push the board into a serious reflective mode, leading to an environmental analysis of where the organization stands. This process may very well cause the board to take a strategic look to the future, identifying the key organizational issues the new CEO will face in the next five to ten years. Then the board can ask, What are the leadership requirements we need for the future? The board should develop a list of priorities it's seeking in a new CEO. What key areas of knowledge, what key skills, and what type of personality should this person have? From this process, a professional and personal profile starts to emerge.

If the board has difficulty developing this profile, the problem may be general board dysfunction or lack of consensus about the organization's direction. The CEO may be hired to resolve the conflict, and the organization risks letting an outsider determine the direction of the public trust. Ideally, a board will resolve its conflicts before hiring a CEO. In some situations, a board may need to bring in an outside consultant to help resolve these conflicts before beginning the CEO recruitment process.

## Seeking Help with Recruiting

A variety of good resources are available to help organizations recruit CEOs. Psychological testing can help reveal the true characteristics and key personality strengths of an individual.

Service organization leaders have come to recognize the importance of testing because they have become aware of the limitations of most job interviews. What is now commonly understood as the "first five-minute impression" can sway the interviewer for or against the candidate. However, the answers to the questions, "Can the person do it?" and "Will the person do it?" and "Does the person fit our culture?" require more sophisticated approaches to exploring a person's match for a position. "An accurate understanding of a person's abilities, motives that drive working, and indicators of job satisfaction dwarf experience and expertise as primary factors in a good position match," according to David Lichter, chief operating officer of Growth Design.

## Recruiting with Direction and a Plan

The CEO's job is to represent the board in day-to-day operations. Therefore, it is important that the selected individual represents and understands the direction in which the board is going. The board needs to map out this direction before starting the recruitment process and communicate this very clearly to candidates for the CEO position.

It is important for the board to empower a point person to lead the recruitment process—a person who will coordinate effectively with any outside consulting firm while ensuring that the board stays closely involved and maintains its position as the final decision maker when a CEO is hired. There is a danger that board members may, for lack of time, delegate the recruitment process to an outside consultant or a committee independent of the board and not participate fully in the process. Then, at the point of decision, board members may realize their CEO candidate is not exactly the person they need because the criteria for selection did not reflect the board's current direction.

A consultant can provide valuable assistance during CEO recruiting. However, the expertise and objectivity an experienced outside consultant can bring to recruiting may broaden the scope of applicants initially, help in narrowing the list of appropriate candidates, and guide the board toward a decision focused on the organization's needs and objectives. Although board members may be distracted by a variety of special interests and relationships, the consultant can assist in targeting a candidate who meets pre-established criteria. Associations and other resources listed in the Resource section of the Appendix can be excellent referral sources for prospective consultants.

A prospective CEO profile can be a tool for an outside human resource professional to use in initiating the search process; however, boards should be wary of traditional search firms and should ask whether the prospective firm is capable of finding the kind of person the board has identified. Boards should scrutinize the firm's ability and track record carefully in relation to the kind of person being targeted, the networks in which that person may be found, and the search firm's experience in those networks. The conventional approach of going to someone who fits the mold of the traditional CEO by identifying the best leaders in the field may, in fact, result in a poor choice. Some search firms are placing people in transforming organizations who may have been ideal for the job last year but are not necessarily good for this year or for the future.

An example of a CEO search that worked well with the involvement of an outside consultant is an inner-city service organization. When the board of this organization learned that its current executive director would be retiring, they realized they had a limited amount of time to commit to the substantial amount of legwork involved in an executive search process; yet the board wanted to remain involved with the hiring decision. With this in mind, they decided to hire the services of a consulting company to coordinate the recruitment process and bring forth several candidates for final interviews with a newly designated search committee.

The board of directors felt it was essential that members of this search committee be vital, active members of the community, with exposure to the organization and its child-focused programs. Strong personal belief in preserving and supporting the mission of the organization was essential, as was recognition of the changing needs of social service organizations. Committee members would need to understand that hiring an experienced and competent executive director with the ability to advance the organization and meet its resource needs was a priority and therefore worth the personal time and attention the search would require.

The board of directors decided that the ideal committee composition would be approximately six members, with representation from the board, staff, and at least one external constituent. Under the direction of the chair of the board's personnel committee, the search committee needed to exhibit leadership and involvement in the search process.

The search committee chair met with the consultants to communicate clear expectations and responsibilities from the beginning, outline the organization's needs and objectives, and develop a work plan and timeline. The consultants conducted the initial steps in the recruitment process, including advertising and networking, collecting and analyzing resumes, and conducting the initial interviews of candidates. In order to keep the organization informed throughout the process, the consultants sent biweekly progress reports to the search committee and communicated regularly with its chairperson. Once several strong candidates had been identified, an executive search summary packet, with all crucial information, was given to the search committee. The committee then conducted the final interviews themselves, brought the top candidate to the board, and, ultimately, made the final hiring decision.

In this successful example, the board members on the search committee stayed closely involved and provided the necessary leadership in the recruitment process. They set clear expectations and objectives with the consultants at the beginning of the executive search, appointed the chair of the search committee as the communication liaison between the committee and consultants, and remained in close contact throughout the process. The board of directors still owned the process of hiring their new executive director but without the time-consuming daily work involved in a search process.

## Supporting the New CEO

Once the candidate is chosen, board members need to develop a plan for orienting and supporting the new CEO. This plan may include appropriate introductions and guidelines for building the proper relationships between the new person and the existing board members. These steps are essential in order to build an effective team. The CEO needs to feel a partnership with the board. At the beginning of this relationship, the stage can be set for the evaluation process with the CEO and board working together to establish goals and agenda points that will be part of a performance evaluation in the future. During the first year after being hired, the CEO should visit all board members individually.

If the board and CEO are not working together from the beginning, the result can be disastrous. As an example, a small midwestern university hired a new president who determined independently, without consulting the board, that the university needed to go through a major transformation. He took the institution in a new direction, did not tune into the target market, did not understand the organization's history, and almost took the university under. Much of the responsibility for this problem was with the dysfunctional board that had not articulated expectations for the CEO or set up a process for regular communication. When the board finally realized what was going on, it fired the CEO and appointed an interim president who was closely aligned with the board. Eventually, working together, a new president and the board did, in fact, determine that transformation was necessary; however, they had consensus on the direction they needed to go, so the university thrived under new leadership.

In practice, the board needs to actively support the CEO through its agenda setting, planning, and policymaking. This entails regular communication and articulation of the organization's mission and direction. During times of great change, it is particularly important for the board and the CEO to be moving toward the same goals and to fully understand the steps necessary to achieve those goals. The

CEO-board relationship is in trouble when communication stops, when the board finds itself surprised at steps the CEO has implemented, or realizes that operations are not reflecting policy and mission. The stage should be set for a positive and productive board-CEO relationship when the CEO is hired, with the mechanisms for communication and evaluation being established at that time.

## Ending Relationships Properly

If a relationship was worth starting properly, it's worth ending properly. In most instances, it's best to view the person leaving the CEO position, for whatever reason, as a valuable asset to the organization in the future. Consequently, it's best for everyone involved if the board focuses on ending the CEO relationship in as positive a way as possible.

In many cases, setting up events for saying good-byes and getting closure are very appropriate, especially if the retiring CEO is moving to a different part of the country. In cases where conflict has occurred, resolving those conflicts before the CEO departs is desirable for everyone involved. This process may not occur at board meetings but in smaller group meetings, with the goal of healing wounds so that both the departing CEO and the board members who are staying feel a sense of closure and resolution. Even in the worst of situations, if at all possible boards may acknowledge the departing CEO for contributions made to the organization. The result will be a healthier organization that is ready to move on and start the process of hiring a new CEO in a positive atmosphere.

It is also best if the departing CEO participates in an exit interview and evaluation so that board members can learn from the CEO's experience with the organization, especially in short-lived or difficult situations. Board members might ask the departing CEO, "Why didn't this work?" and "What can we do to alleviate this kind of situation in the future?"

Sometimes boards consider retaining the retiring CEO in another position, perhaps as a fundraiser, because of the relationships that have been established. Boards should be cautious and think this step through carefully before proceeding. In some situations, the retiring CEO who stays around can be inhibiting as the new CEO strives to gain control of the operation and establish relationships.

## Handling Interim Leadership Carefully

CEO searches can run from a year to eighteen months—or sometimes longer. How the board manages the organization in this interim is a key issue. Many boards want to cut this time period short because of pressures to have a new CEO in place; however, in moving too quickly, boards may be compromising the thoroughness of the recruiting process.

This is an important time period in the life of any organization, and each situation is different. Organizations may flounder or flourish during this crucial interim period. An announced retirement typically allows a window of opportunity for pursuing a thorough hiring process while keeping the current CEO in place. A resignation (whether unexpected or requested) or difficult health situation may present the necessity for an interim leader. This time period may allow the board to go through the careful selection process of finding the proper CEO.

Although some boards may feel pressure to find a new CEO as quickly as possible, it may be wisest for boards to have a temporary leader in place and take an adequate amount of time to find the right person. An interim period can give the board a clearer vision of the kind of CEO they want and may become a very positive strategy for change; however, waiting too long with a temporary leader in place may impede the positive momentum of a changing organization. The board needs to strive for an appropriate balance between lingering too long without a permanent CEO and allowing enough time for a thorough search.

## Timing Leadership Changes Appropriately

The engagement model of leadership emphasizes the recruitment of strong leadership, both on the board and in an organization's management. The process of transformation starts with leadership. The leaders of an organization must be willing and able to envision change and must also possess the courage to lead the process. Competent management needs to be in place to implement the process, but the board and management leaders must be there to oversee and persuade. Once the roles of leadership and management have been established, the process selected for change work can begin.

For example, in a planning process with a college board and senior management, it was realized that a number of changes were needed to transform the college into a higher-quality institution for its new target markets. New talents were needed on the board, a different experience level was needed on the management team, and enhancements were needed in the faculty and administration in order for the college to get to the point being set as the standard. During initial discussions as the college embarked on the transformation process, it was determined that the right leaders had to be in place before the organization could move forward toward its goals. Without the right leaders it looked unlikely that the organization could get where it wanted to go. So early in the transformation process the college made significant changes at its highest leadership levels, and these leaders were able to take the institution to the next step.

This is a common scenario during transformation, as boards make sometimes difficult but essential decisions about the kind of leadership needed to carry the organization through the process of change. Leaders who were excellent during a period of maintaining the status quo may not have the right skills and experience to lead effectively in volatile times of dramatic change. Effective boards need to lead their organizations through these kinds of decisions and personnel changes, both at the board and management levels.

## Questions for Reflection

What is your board's profile of an effective CEO? Of an effective board member? Do you have specific, measurable performance objectives in place for your CEO and your board members?

What is your current CEO-board relationship? Who is in control?

Does the CEO of your organization have the same leadership style and professional background as his or her predecessor? Is this style appropriate for your current environment?

What plans do you have in place for recruiting a new CEO if the need should arise?

Do more than half of your current board members share the same professional, cultural, or socioeconomic background, or run into each other during the course of their daily lives?

What plans do you have for ongoing board member recruitment and development? Do you have a committee looking at this process on an ongoing basis?

How well does your board understand and represent your marketplace? Do you think that your board is diverse enough to fully understand the constituency you serve?

What plans do you have for successful beginnings and endings of both CEO and board relationships?

*Chapter Two*

# Preparation for High Performance

The best preparation for good work tomorrow is to
do good work today.

*Elbert Hubbard*

In this chapter, board members will learn that to ensure high performance on the board they need to attend board meetings, carefully prepare before meetings, participate in follow-up after meetings, and be involved in ongoing communication between meetings with the CEO and other board members.

Joy is in her fourth year of a six-year term as a board member of a national association. When she was recruited, she had participated as a member of the association for a number of years. She prepares for quarterly board meetings by reading the literature sent in advance by the CEO through the organization's Web site, visiting personally with the CEO before the meeting through e-mail and telephone, and participating regularly in association seminars—a core service of the organization. She comes to the board meeting with notes, questions, and prepared thoughts to respond to the items in the agenda. She is excited about her role and is perceived by her peers and the CEO as an effective board leader. Overall, Joy has found her board experience to be a rewarding one.

Wayne is a very talented community leader who is also CEO of a major corporation. He is sought-after and sits on numerous boards in the community where the corporate headquarters is located. For the last three years, he has been a board member of a significant performing arts group, but he has attended only one board meeting during his tenure because of numerous conflicts; however, he has lent his name to a major fundraising effort and, as a result, the organization has received some significant gifts and grants. Yet the organization is not just in dire need of funds but of planning and preparing for its future. Currently, this arts group is undergoing a major transformation, focusing on developing new resources—both people and dollars—to fulfill a dramatically larger vision. Wayne observes that although he feels he has helped, he hasn't made any significant impact on the organization's planning and policy formation. As a result, his board experience has not been very rewarding, personally or professionally. He feels overextended and is considering resigning from the board.

Board members are asked to join the leadership group that oversees tax-exempt organizations in order to represent the public interest and the good of the community. As nonprofit organizations become more sophisticated and as the arena becomes more competitive, preparation is clearly an important aspect of each board member's role. In a "some-will-get-stronger" world, some organizations will dissolve, some will be acquired by other nonprofits or by for-profit organizations, and some will transform themselves into stronger service organizations. The organizations that grow stronger during times of change will have well-prepared and committed board members. In the midst of this changing and uncertain environment, it will be essential for board members to spend more time preparing, communicating, and interacting with other board members and also management.

The engagement model of board governance profiles board members on fully functioning, results-oriented boards who adequately prepare for their multiple roles as planners, policymakers, marketers, resource developers, and evaluators. In a fast-paced and busy world, it is important that board members know what options are available to them as they pursue these roles and what efficient steps can be taken to prepare for board meetings, as well as for ongoing work between meetings.

On many not-for-profit boards, it is obvious to board members, their colleagues, and senior management that some board members prepare more fully than others. Some board members have sporadic attendance at meetings or come late and leave early. At times, their comments and participation levels reveal a lack of knowledge about the problem or subject on the table, or their comments are redundant because they are raising issues that have already been resolved at earlier meetings. Time after time, board members are told that the subject of their concern was covered in the packet of materials sent prior to the meeting or was voted on after they left the last meeting.

In contrast, the more engaged board members arrive early, joining fellow board members in conversation in preparation for the meeting and bringing pertinent materials for use during the board session. They bring notes on their prepared thoughts; they take notes during the meeting; they organize notes afterward for use in subsequent small groups and as a reminder of tasks they intend to accomplish.

In well-managed organizations, the CEO, usually in concert with the board chair, needs to develop a procedure for communicating with board members in the interim between meetings. Although this communication is important and guides board members in their preparation, much more can and should be done to prepare for high-performance leadership.

Nonprofit boards are increasingly using technology to maintain communication. CEOs are sending regular e-mail reports to board members, and board members are communicating with each other about specific tasks or issues of concern. In addition, many boards, particularly those following the engagement model, are holding committee meetings in the interim between board meetings. In times of fast-paced change, where boards need to stay on top of developing plans, ongoing communication and in-depth preparation are crucial.

For example, a social service agency providing care for developmentally disabled individuals realized it was not making the best use of its talented board of directors. A new executive director had come on board and wanted to find ways to tap into all of the board's talents. The director's first step in improving board communications was a proposed change in technology. The board had a national membership, with directors residing all over the country. Therefore, it needed to improve communication during the time between meetings. Consequently, every board member was outfitted with a laptop computer. The cost of these computers was well worth the improved communication, which strengthened the board's involvement and encouraged invaluable input on a regular basis.

In another case, a model of a well-prepared board is a large national social service system that serves people with severe mental and physical disabilities. Fully engaged board members continually study trends in the organization's field through literature disseminated by the CEO. The board meets for three days quarterly. In addition to their board discussions, board members visit programs, observe activities, and hear briefings by staff. Between quarterly meetings, board members communicate regularly with each other and the organization's senior management. Committee meetings frequently take place via the organization's Web site or conference calls.

The board has a regular annual agenda related to reviewing all policies in an orderly fashion. At the end of board meetings, each board member has tasks to report on at the next meeting. The CEO also commits to follow-up. These commitments are tracked on the Web site until the next meeting. All this preparation and follow-through paints an impressive picture of a thoroughly informed and prepared board that is extremely effective in leading this highly successful organization.

There are great benefits to an organization when a board prepares properly. Key indicators that senior management and board members regularly review and that are based on agreed-upon plans are being exceeded. The organization's endowment has grown rapidly and is significant almost beyond the needs of the organization, signaling great potential for growth. The organization is currently going through a transformation process under a revised mission, a new vision, and a refined set of value statements—all reviewed, considered, and approved by the board in partnership with senior management. The organization is considered a leader in its field and is gaining market share nationally.

In another example, the board of a local cultural organization met monthly, with each meeting lasting at least two hours and frequently longer. Even though the president of the organization regularly distributed an agenda and resource material prior to the meeting, board members typically did not bother to read the material, so they spent a significant amount of time at meetings reviewing material. Members were frequently late for meetings, left meetings early, or didn't attend at all. The importance of their board activity was obviously very diminished in the eyes of board members.

Needless to say, this organization was floundering without adequate direction, particularly when their marketplace started to go through dramatic changes. Consultants asked the board to reflect on the effectiveness of their meetings as they related to the organization's current problems. Then, working with the CEO, the board developed a new and more effective approach to board meetings. They established timed agendas and held fewer but more substantial and focused meetings, during which each board member played a significant role. Board members became more energized and enthusiastic about meetings when they realized their input was needed and made a difference.

There are no hard-and-fast rules about how often or how long boards should meet, how board meetings should be organized, or how much preparation should be expected of board members; however, boards can expect to work more intensely during periods of change. Boards need to establish working procedures based on the needs of the organization and related to the kinds of outcomes that are targeted in order for the board to meet its responsibilities in overseeing the public trust. In anticipation of change, a board's structure and organization need to be carefully reviewed by board members in consultation with the CEO.

## Performing Specific Functions

During times of change, virtually all board members should be expected to participate in small-group or action-team meetings and to work with the CEO and other leaders on various projects and tasks that will carry the transformation process forward. As this occurs, board members will be asked to perform specific functions such as

- Learning about the market through careful listening
- Thinking strategically in groups
- Setting performance goals
- Understanding market trends and tying them to organizational change and the implementation of new services or programming
- Playing important roles in group processes
- Bringing their own outside experience and expertise to decision making or connecting the organization to other professionals
- Assessing and monitoring processes
- Making decisions for the good of the institution and the greater constituent community

Each of these functions demands preparation, including knowing the organization, the environment, and the issues, in addition to understanding the abilities and interests of the group of leaders assembled, including board members and senior managers.

Figure 2.1 illustrates a sample process boards may go through in order to achieve programming changes. The chart shows how a board may begin the change process by thinking about the changes.

## Figure 2.1.  Thinking and Planning Flow Chart

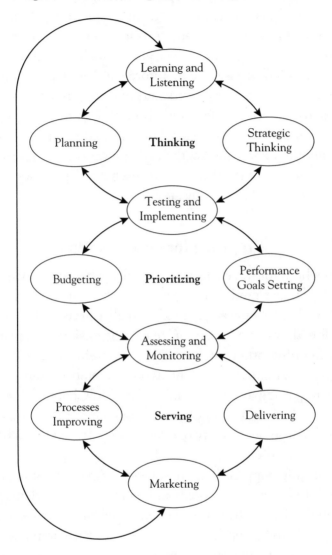

Thinking about changes involves learning and listening, thinking strategically, and beginning continuous planning. Next comes the prioritization of steps leading to implementation, including budgeting and setting performance goals. Finally, there is a change in service, which needs to be monitored and assessed, resulting in an improvement in the process and delivery, as well as related changes in marketing. The arrows show how all these steps are interrelated and affect each other. There is no direct path from one step to another. For instance, the early process of learning and listening is essential in the thinking process but also provides valuable input into eventual marketing efforts.

## Preparing for Group Roles

Leaders who want to be effective and fully engaged in board activities should understand that they need to take some time when they join a board to become acquainted with all aspects of the organization before they begin to participate in policymaking and planning, and in fulfilling other vital roles. A comprehensive orientation process can be immensely helpful as board members prepare for active board participation. (See more detail in Chapter One on effective board orientations.) Once integrated into the board, leaders will need to assume a variety of roles (discussed next) for a healthy group process to occur.

Leadership happens in groups. Leadership does not happen in isolated situations. Therefore board members should demand appropriate leadership from each other, as reflected in roles that are played within the group. The people who play these important roles might be called regulators, facilitators, information givers, nurturers, and contrarians.

### Regulators

The regulators oversee the agenda, the outcomes, and the pace of meetings, including the process followed during meetings. These leaders ensure that all items relevant to moving the transformation process forward are covered during meetings and are responsible for keeping discussions on track and targeted. If no one fills this role, meetings will meander and be much less productive. Board members may leave these meetings frustrated, feeling that their time was wasted and their efforts were unproductive. The board chair is often considered the champion of this role, but others must fill in when the chair is weak in this area. Board chairs are typically expected to assume the regulator role, but sometimes an experienced and well-meaning but disorganized chair doesn't keep the meeting moving and lets discussions go on too long, resulting in wasted time and unproductive meetings. Regulating the timing of the agenda is a key ingredient in efficient board meetings, but not all chairs have that ability. When that is the case, someone on the board needs to fill that role or there will be a significant void on the board.

### Facilitators

Leaders who are facilitators can interpret what is being said for the group and advance the discussion toward consensus and decisions. The facilitator knows when the group is likely to be at the point of decision, can ask pointed questions to lead the group toward decisions, and can assist the group in negotiating the appropriate steps for arriving at the best decision. Crucial decisions need to be made at board meetings during the transformation process. Actually making these decisions sometimes becomes a major obstacle during meetings unless a facilitator can lead discussions to a decisive point. Facilitators are essential because they make things happen. Facilitation can be as simple as asking the right question at the right time to guide the group discussion.

### Information Givers

Leaders who give information provide current and vital information and interpretation during the group process to aid in board member preparation and quality decision making. In a fascinating book, *The Tipping Point* (Gladwell, 2000), the author, Malcolm Gladwell, discusses a word from the Yiddish, "maven," which means "one who accumulates knowledge." He says, "In recent years, economists have spent a great deal of time studying mavens, for the obvious reason that if marketplaces depend on information, the people with the most information must be the most important" (p. 60).

Thus mavens are extremely crucial to the operation of a successful board. Without accurate, in-depth information, good decisions cannot be reached. Up-to-date information is especially important on an ongoing basis during transformation because markets and strategies are in a constant state of flux. The agenda of each board meeting should include time for the "information giver" to update members on changes in the industry, the marketplace, and the organization and its status.

### Nurturers

Nurturers are leaders who encourage and support other leaders during meetings, providing positive reinforcement and interpretation. Board members need support and encouragement as they express opinions and make decisions in a high-risk, changing environment. In a highly charged atmosphere of change, it is all too easy for hurt feelings and negative interactions among board members to inhibit a board's productivity. Deciding on crucial changes for an organization can generate emotions such as fear, anger, and frustration—all of which may disable a board's decision-making process, blocking the organization's forward motion. The nurturer plays an essential role in helping board members support each other and respect each other during the sometimes tense decision-making process. Without nurturers, some board members may be reticent to express their opinions and may even stop coming to meetings altogether.

### Contrarians

Contrarians are leaders who don't always think within the boundaries of the current situation. Peter Drucker (1995) once expressed the opinion that a board decision that is unanimous should be delayed. His point was that a board without dissent may not be fully considering the implications of its decision. It frequently takes a "contrarian" thinker to generate the kind of debate that leads to solid decision making. Contrary thinkers are critical to the transformation process because new ground is being broken on a continuing basis. Contrarians can be refreshing and energizing, building the strategic tension within a group that sets the stage for creative and innovative decision making. If no one is willing to think differently or take a risk with a new idea, change cannot take place. Contrarians are agents of change.

### Other Roles

There are many other roles that board members may assume in conjunction with these basic roles. For instance, on most boards there are "buyers" and "sellers." Buyers are essential because they have a greater ability to bring in resources for the organization than sellers do. Every nonprofit board needs members with this ability.

The need for board members to assume effective leadership roles is intensified in times of change because the stakes are higher, as are the tensions about the future. As a result, group roles need to be pursued very carefully. In some cases, board members naturally assume a role (or sometimes more than one role); in others, the board president and CEO may need to make it clear to board members what roles they are being expected to fill on the board. If one or more of these roles is not represented, the board may be weakened and hindered from making necessary changes during the transformation process.

As an example of how important each role is on a board of directors, the board of a growing religious organization found itself in a state of almost constant conflict. The climate at board meetings was confrontational, and meetings were not productive. Members would leave meetings feeling great stress and frequently with hurt feelings. Conflicts were not resolved and were carried over into committee work and future board meetings. Despite their deep commitment to the organization, board members were missing meetings, and some valuable members even left the board.

Board members were at a loss as to what was missing. Many of the standard board roles were being filled. The board had plenty of information, and several members were filling the contrarian role. So the board brought in consultants who identified the need for nurturers in the group. Through small-group activity, current board members were taught to nurture each other, and some new board members were brought on board specifically to assume the nurturing role. Soon the board began to work together as a stronger team, and members actually started to leave meetings arm-in-arm. Needless to say, the board's work was much more productive and the organization started to thrive.

Leaders preparing for high-performance leadership should think through which roles and functions are missing from their organization's board meetings and small-group sessions. Preparing may include thinking about how to help bring these important functions to the meeting and how to participate to make meetings more functional, efficient, and productive.

When selecting new board members, boards may want to consider these role functions. A nominating team in partnership with the CEO could assess what group roles are already present on the board and what voids exist that make the group less functional. Profiles of prospective board members should be part of a well-planned board recruitment strategy to solve any identified role voids on the board.

Existing board members, having thought through these important group roles, can adjust their own roles to fill voids and play multiple roles when they recognize what the group needs in order to function successfully. None of these roles can be filled effectively without careful thought and study before meetings take place. Board members who are aware of these roles and act to make sure they are filled become invaluable assets to the group. A fully functioning board is one goal of the engagement model of board governance.

## Preparing in a Variety of Ways

Preparation needs to occur throughout the periods between meetings. Committee meetings and social functions where constituents are gathered frequently offer ideal opportunities for preparation. These gatherings provide a place for board members to ask questions related to evaluating services, constituent attitudes, environmental trends, and organizational capabilities. Committee chairs can set the stage for this kind of exchange of information.

Reading current literature related to the organization's service and leadership's role is another important way of staying abreast of trends in the field or industry. The Resource section in the Appendix lists current books, periodicals, and trade journals read by organization leaders in the areas of health, religion, education, and social service. Subscribing to several of these leading periodicals will help organization leaders identify trends, issues, and directions of similar organizations.

The most effective board members stay in touch with their CEOs and vice versa. Although CEOs are busy, an occasional call or visit to listen to what goals are being achieved and what issues are emerging for the next board meeting provides a valuable base for board work. It also provides a time to support the work of the CEO—the person who carries the vision and mission of the board into the community and implements the policies and plans of board members.

Typically, a good CEO sends board members the agenda and appropriate materials in advance of meetings. These materials need to be relevant to current organizational plans and issues and organized so that pertinent information can be accessed easily during meetings. Each agenda item can highlight what is being expected of the board members for this item, such as commenting, critiquing, networking, raising questions, and engaging in strategic thinking.

Materials sent in advance of a board meeting could include the following:

- A timed agenda that includes the item to be discussed, the time allotted for that discussion, and the board member assigned to lead the discussion of that particular agenda item
- Financial reports indicating results versus goals
- Measurements against best-of-class indicators chosen by the board and the CEO

- Quality reviews and customer satisfaction reports
- Relevant market research
- Service reports and evaluations from various parts of the organization
- Plan results
- Committee or task force reports with recommendations and exhibits
- Issues for consideration and relevant data for analysis

Some CEOs also develop interim reports or regular communication tools, frequently transmitted via e-mail, for board members and other key leaders to keep them informed. During significant organizational changes, communication must be stronger, at a higher level, and more interpretive.

Draft resolutions from committees or task groups ought to be part of the material that board members study in advance of meetings. Discussion of these resolutions can be scheduled early in the board meeting's agenda because they imply decisions. At the beginnings of meetings, efficient boards frequently work on decisions, allowing time for related planning and strategic thinking to take place as the meeting progresses. This is especially important in a time of change so that key decisions are made early in a meeting in a timely fashion and do not get set aside, which might hold the organization back at a crucial time.

Sometimes board meetings can be very effective if they are targeted toward one specific goal rather than aimed at covering the waterfront. Exhibit 2.1 is an actual board meeting agenda, which is targeted toward a particular goal—in this case a board assessment. This board had gone through a formal board assessment process, and the meeting reflected in the agenda was organized to present the data collected to the board and give the board an opportunity to react and move forward. Each step on the agenda is timed, and steps are presented in a logical sequence, leading to the final step of planning. A carefully honed agenda such as this one will carry the board efficiently through a productive board meeting leading to a specific goal.

Active, involved boards target their agendas toward change and will expect the full and intense involvement of the board. This can only happen when board members have taken the time to consider issues and prepare for strategic discussions. Time is of the essence at board meetings; when members are prepared, meetings run more efficiently and are much more productive.

In addition to studying any materials submitted prior to board meetings, busy board members can enhance their preparation by regularly considering key questions and issues related to the organization they are serving. The following list outlines some preparations and questions that may help board members and CEOs prepare for meetings and develop meeting agendas. Even the most dedicated, engaged board members have some time limitations, so taking the time before a meeting to tackle just a few of these issues will greatly enhance a board member's contributions to meetings.

### Exhibit 2.1.  Board Assessment Agenda

| | |
|---|---|
| 1:30 P.M. | Opening Prayer |
| | Introduction of Assessment Report |
| 1:35 P.M. | Presentation of Assessment Data |
| 2:15 P.M. | Dialogue, Questions, and Comments |
| 2:30 P.M. | Small Group Assignments to React to Report |
| 3:00 P.M. | Report from Small Groups |
| 3:15 P.M. | Break |
| 3:30 P.M. | Groups Reconvene |
| 4:00 P.M. | Small Group Reports |
| 4:30 P.M. | Synthesis |
| 5:00 P.M. | Research and Planning Process |
| 5:30 P.M. | Closing |

- A review of the current strategic plan, including mission statement, statements of values or principles, a defined vision or corporate direction, and goals and strategies

- A review of reports that indicate the status of current plans, financial sheets for comparisons and analysis, year-to-date balance sheets and cash flow statements, and benchmarks with regard to competitors and best-of-class providers

- A review of literature, studies, and reports on trends, issues, and current research in the industry and the marketplace being served by the organization

- A review of the marketplace the organization serves, its profile, and the needs and wants of constituents-customers

Addressing the following questions can also be helpful:

What market (if any) do you represent, and what issues and concerns are harbored in that market that can be articulated as the board works on plans and policy?

What are the challenges, concerns, and issues the CEO and management team are currently facing? What plans or solutions are they contemplating to deal with these issues?

What are other board members thinking about the organization's plans and results?

What is the overall board agenda for transformation? What do the CEO and senior management perceive as the most pressing needs of the organization?

What have you given financially to the organization? What expectations are there on the part of your peers and the CEO for further philanthropy? Where are opportunities for high-impact giving? What networking can you do to encourage philanthropy from other sources?

What other resource solutions are being used in addition to philanthropy? Is there a plan for the use and integration of additional resource solutions, both short term and long term? (See Chapter Six for more information on resource solutions.)

## Following Up for Further Leadership

After meetings, it is important to recall commitments made by the group and by individual board members and managers during the meeting. These commitments require follow-up in order to capitalize on the full potential of board members, the CEO, and the management group. Timely communication between the CEO and board colleagues keeps members engaged and motivated, illustrating to everyone involved that there is interest and commitment on both sides. It is, however, important to ensure that follow-up materials are targeted and appropriate for the tasks at hand. Too much paperwork or irrelevant materials can become overwhelming and misdirect preparation, wasting valuable time and diluting the preparation process.

In summary, in nonprofit organizations, particularly when transformation is in progress or anticipated, board membership is serious business, and this understanding needs to be emphasized during the recruiting process. Board members are not merely names on a letterhead. They should understand that they need to attend meetings regularly, be prepared for meetings, and become actively engaged during meetings. The result will be a fully functioning, completely engaged board and a truly rewarding board experience for members.

## Questions for Reflection

Is the importance of preparation emphasized in your board's recruitment process?

Does your board have a preparation plan, and is it reviewed regularly for effectiveness?

For what projects, plans, policies, and activities does your board need to prepare?

How do you rate your board, based on preparedness? Do some board members seem to participate and attend meetings more than others? What steps can be taken to encourage better preparation and attendance?

Do you spend less time preparing for a board meeting than you spend attending the board meeting?

How does good preparation enhance your performance as a board member? How do you rate your performance based on preparedness?

Are all the group functions outlined in this chapter filled on your board? If not, how can you add needed board functions to your existing board?

# Chapter Three

# Policy Review and Formation

The future never just happened. It was created.

*Will and Ariel Durant*

In this chapter, board members will gain a deeper understanding of how policy is made, what their role in setting and reviewing policy is, and how policy decision making connects to an organization's day-to-day operations.

Sam is on the board of directors of a Catholic liberal arts college in his community. During the era of apartheid in South Africa, Sam and his fellow board members faced the challenging question of whether or not college investment policy should prohibit investments in South African companies. Today he faces a similar policy question as it relates to the tobacco industry. Can a Catholic college, owned by a religious order and promoting holistic health and service to humankind, justify investments in an industry that contributes to a major medical crisis, along with the resulting health care costs? He presents his concern to the board and opens the door for an animated but productive discussion of the college's investment policies. As a result, the board establishes a policy forbidding these kinds of investments.

Sally is a board member of a national, nonprofit, long-term care organization that owns a group of nursing homes; the facilities contribute a percentage of their revenues to the national organization. Several of the nursing home affiliates throughout the country are losing money and are unable to contribute to the national organization. The board deliberated about establishing a policy of selling affiliate organizations because they drain resources from the other entities. Board discussion indicated that many affiliates were concerned about backing down on other affiliate organizations when they were in need of support, yet they also recognized the need to consider the concerns of contributing affiliates. As a result, a policy was established that allows the nonpaying affiliates to remain members for two years while they try to improve their financial situation. Meanwhile, the board provides financial consultation to these affiliates. If at the end of two years these nonpaying affiliate organizations are still unable to pay, the established policy directs that they will be sold.

Setting policy has always been a key board activity. Firm, well-articulated policies are integral to the successful operation of any organization; however, when an organization is in a mode of change, an ongoing monitoring of policies is essential. In the past, many boards viewed setting policy as their sole domain, perhaps addressed once a year or so, whereas the engagement model of board governance recommends that board policy decisions involve a continuous review approach, in partnership with the CEO and senior management. In addition, the engagement model calls for board members to go beyond setting policy and become actively involved in the planning, positioning, and developing of resources that spring from policy making.

*Policy* can be defined as a directional statement that answers these questions: What will we do?, Why are we doing it this way?, and What principles do we have that direct our board decisions? Policy statements are usually based on principles or values held by members of the board and are associated with the core purpose of the organization.

Board members should understand the difference between policy decisions and strategic or tactical decisions. Policy answers the "what" and "why" questions; strategy answers the "how" question.

Tactics deal with activity and usually answer the "when, where, who" and "at-what-cost" questions.

For example, a college may decide that it will only provide residential-based services because of its mission to create a complete learning environment for students. This is a policy decision with "what" and "why" components. The "how" question might be answered by the strategic decision to establish a high-quality campus where students live and study. Resulting tactics may lead to a computer with Internet access in every student's room and interactive video in classrooms for outside expertise that enhances faculty instruction.

## Prioritizing Policies

Policies set the framework for day-to-day decision making that is related to procedures, processes, and operational activity. They guide the very core of the organization as its staff provides services and products to the community of target-market constituents. It can be argued that there is no more important role for a board than to set policies that guide the organization. This approach certainly reflects the policy-centered model for effective board leadership, as recommended by John Carver and Miriam Mayhew Carver in their guide, *Basic Principles of Policy Governance* (1996a).

In times of change, however, boards need to recognize that policies cannot be static and need to be adjusted to take account of the changing environment, the changing attitudes of leaders, and the changing perceptions, attitudes, needs, and desires of constituents or customers. Policies reflect a community in motion. The process of change calls for ongoing policy evaluation and revision.

The dynamic nature of policy formation for boards confronting change demands timely reviews related to current policies, plans, and implementation, along with continual diligence and decision making. This motion and demand for policy adjustment can create significant conflict among board members. Great care needs to be taken when recruiting members to discuss the organization and its current policies in order to prevent eventual insurmountable con-flicts because of differing values. This is a challenge for most orga-nizations because they need diverse viewpoints in the process of creating effective policies. However, basic value congruence is im-portant to the creation of a strong board that can establish strong policies. It is healthy for board members from diverse perspectives to express significant differences concerning planning and strategic options, but their underlying value systems should reflect the values of the organization.

It is important for board members to become thoroughly in-formed about board policies, including the history of policy devel-opment, when they join the board. Learning about policies does not just mean reading a hand-out of policy statements. Real policy un-derstanding takes place when board members talk directly to the staff members who implement policies and to constituents who are directly affected by policies. These opportunities should be part of an orientation agenda for each new board member. Then each board meeting should include some aspect of policy review, partic-ularly in areas where change is taking place. All policies should be subject to regular board review. Serious problems can emerge if this does not happen.

For instance, it had been many years since a small church board had reviewed its policies related to insurance and liability, even though its programs had gone through significant expansion and change. One new program was a day care center; that's where a problem developed. A staff member was accused of inappropriately touching a child, and the parents were threatening to sue the church and the church council. The church council was caught by surprise and realized it had no idea what its policies and insurance coverage were related to this incident. They had overlooked the possibility of reviewing their policies as their programming changed. The result of this negligence had placed the church in a serious sit-uation that was actually threatening its existence. Fortunately, in this case the church was able to settle the problem outside of court; the church then launched a thorough review of its policies as they related to programming changes.

In another situation, the board of directors at a growing university was in the process of eliminating programs that no longer met the changing needs and interests of students; however, a belated policy review revealed that the faculty needed to approve all program changes. The faculty was reluctant to discard some courses, and an unpleasant confrontation ensued between the faculty and the board. If the board had reviewed its policies as they related to course elimination before taking action, this unfortunate disagreement might have been avoided. The board would have been able to lay the groundwork for change and possibly even change the policies involved. Eventually, a compromise was reached with the faculty but not before hard feelings were generated on both sides and the university had lost several key board members and faculty members.

The lessons learned belatedly by the boards in these examples may serve as a warning to all nonprofit boards of directors. Despite the importance of policy setting, many nonprofit boards do not spend enough time establishing and monitoring policies that guide day-to-day management and operational activity. Policy setting and review needs to be a continuing priority on every board's agenda, with even more emphasis as significant changes in programming are taking place.

## Defining CEO and Board Roles
## in Policy Formation

Traditionally, the CEO, as the board's day-to-day representative, is responsible for executing policy, and the board is responsible for setting it. However, in a changing environment CEOs and boards need to work together very closely in determining how policies should evolve in response to changes.

CEOs may conduct research related to policy on behalf of the board, sometimes examining what others in the industry are doing in the areas of policies being considered for establishment or change. CEOs may lead the board toward necessary policy change by presenting the need for policy changes and resolutions, participating in policy discussion, and, in fact, assisting the board in developing policies for review and approval. The effective CEO's role related to policy in a time of change goes beyond discussion and execution; however, everyone needs to understand that the board is still the ultimate policy setter. Certainly, the board does not need to be involved in day-to-day management decisions, but the board should ensure that the CEO's decisions and the organization's activities are reflecting current board policies.

Sometimes the policy-setting roles get reversed or confused in nonprofit organizations. This is especially true when there happens to be a strong leader in the CEO position who may have more longevity than board members rotating in and out. In this situation, the CEO almost assumes the role of board chair, and board members come to meetings to listen to the CEO and respond by providing support to policy requests and direction.

When the board does not monitor the CEO's decisions, CEOs can make decisions that are precedent setting and that go against existing policy. Board members must be diligent in both understanding existing policies and asking this question related to operational decisions: Does this decision reflect our current policy, and is it consistent with what we have decided?

Board members may recognize that their organization's operations do not reflect the board's policies; however, they do not have the right to get involved in operations without CEO approval. If board members do not like how policies are being interpreted and implemented day-to-day, this should be discussed with the CEO and the policies involved clarified. A further step might involve a formal evaluation of the CEO (see Chapter Seven).

## Reviewing Relevant Policies

Policies themselves, unconnected to actual service and day-to-day operations, are usually not very engaging to board members. However, when current and potential policies are connected to day-to-day strategies, they become much more meaningful, exciting, and relevant agenda items. When directions are set and plans are established to implement new services and resource development based on financial modeling, keep in mind that risk management must also be considered because policy change cannot take place without risk. Boards will also need to reevaluate their structure, particularly as it relates to bylaws and to the way the board operates as a public trust.

It is especially important for an organization's board of directors to establish and review policies in the following areas: markets, services, human resources and personnel, operations, and financial resources and pricing. Each will be discussed in the sections that follow.

## Markets

Many policy decisions relate to the marketing of an organization. A review of marketing policies may very well begin with a look at the organization's marketplace and a subsequent evaluation of the relevance of services or products, based on mission and values, perhaps as refined during the transformation process. Boards may need to ask these questions:

Based on our mission and vision of the future, how do we define our market?

What is the profile of our ideal customer or constituent?

What relevant policies do we have that assist us in this thinking process?

These market determinations demand careful thought and statements of policy in order for senior managers to develop strategies and tactics that ensure their successful implementation.

As an example, a neighborhood-based, social service agency board may identify a geographical location as a market emphasis and may set a policy not to discriminate with delivery of its services in that area. The board may also determine special age groups and need areas for which to raise money, seek staff, and procure facilities in order to deliver specific services.

A college may decide to emphasize delivery and programs to students of traditional age. Within that context, the college sets a policy to emphasize a type of student that most suits the college's capabilities. In contrast, another college may decide to provide both on- and off-campus educational services; the college's values, vision, and mission suggest that its market should include students who are unable to attend classes on campus and that its educational service delivery modes are capable of quality service.

A specialty hospital with limited capacity and resources for providing alcohol and drug addiction treatment services may decide, as a policy, to focus its marketing on adults who are willing to self-pay and on those who are referred by recovering alumni.

## Services

Once markets have been determined and needs and desires have been established based on interaction with the constituent or customer, overarching services directed by policy decisions can be established. These services are usually chosen, based on an interpretation of the mission, values, and vision of the organization and its leadership. For instance, colleges may establish policies that they will target only certain markets. Based on these market profiles, one college may only provide liberal arts, undergraduate education using an approved set of programs; another may determine that it will provide undergraduate, liberal arts education and selected preprofessional programs, along with a few graduate degree programs. A community theater board may set a policy that its market is families, including children and teenagers. This decision will limit and define the universe of possible shows the theater will produce.

Throughout the United States, Goodwill Industries organizations have established policies for the collection and resale of clothing and other goods, underscoring the contracting of work as a constructive way to train individuals with disabilities or economic disadvantages. In setting these policies, boards of these organizations have agreed that revenues from entrepreneurial activities will be used to underwrite organizational expenses, to create margins for further capitalization of organizational development, and, at times, to provide incentives and retirement benefits to the individuals who are in training programs at Goodwill. Consequently, these or-ganizations define their services, not only as providing discounted, used items to a disadvantaged market but as providing training to individuals with disabilities.

A crucial policy issue for many nonprofit organizations is how to charge constituents, users, and customers for the services pro-vided. In colleges, for example, tuition becomes a major policy question, with boards discussing areas such as percentage increases, discounted tuition and fees, scholarships, and financial aid for var-ious economic levels. In social service agencies, boards may decide to either not charge certain customers at all or to charge them based on a sliding scale.

A medical center may establish a policy of not providing a certain service, such as heart surgery, because it believes the com-munity is already well covered and would not benefit from an un-necessary and expensive duplication of services. Rather, the hospital decides to allocate its resources toward a stronger obstetrics program—an area underserved in a community with young fami-lies. These policy decisions have an obvious, major impact on the services and programming the hospital provides.

Programming, service, product, and marketing decisions go back to policy and should not be made without a firm understand-ing of how they relate to the established policy. If the CEO or the board is inclined to make a decision that does not reflect current policy, then that policy needs to be reviewed and changed before the new programming or marketing is implemented, or the change should not take place.

## Human Resources and Personnel

Based on changing market forces, policies around the recruitment, training, and support of staff to perform the necessary tasks for service delivery become very important policy issues. Questions related to outsourcing, compensation and rewards, diversity and inclusivity, and tenure are critical policy questions for most organizations in the nonprofit arena.

Over the past two decades, every organization has needed to put into place policies related to drug and alcohol use, sexual harassment, personnel files, and record keeping. Recently, organizations have found themselves addressing policy issues related to workplace violence and electronic communications.

Organizations in the midst of change are particularly vulnerable to employment issues related to endings, mergers, and reorganizations. Boards play a critical role in assisting CEOs in determining whether existing policies and guidelines are up to date. Boards should also assist in policy and guideline application.

As nonprofits move toward transformation, appropriate changes in an organization's personnel force may be crucial, especially when you consider that "people costs" in nonprofits are often 70 to 80 percent of an organization's budget, compared to 6 to 10 percent in a manufacturing firm (Pappas, 1995, p. 38). Organizations today face several critical issues as they attempt to apply policies that affect personnel. The Equal Opportunity Employment (EOE) Act has required clearer and more consistent policies and procedures for hiring, evaluating, and letting go of employees. Other issues may include family and work guidelines, flex hours, parity plans for improving benefits, and development of performance-based compensation and incentive plans. In addition, performance incentive programs for resource development professionals are frequently needed, particularly in light of NSFRE's (National Society for Fund Raising Executives) ethical guidelines that prohibit incentive plans based on money raised.

Nonprofit organizations continue to learn from for-profit businesses on issues related to human resources and labor. Key human resource priorities for organizations going through changes will be recruiting, training, and retaining quality personnel. Currently, higher education, social service, and cultural organizations are beginning to show signs that they are in need of changes in most areas of human resources, predicting intense demands placed on organization leaders as they address these issues.

As organizations are involved in transformation, boards need to ensure the following:

- Human resource or management plans are integrally tied to strategic plans, mission, and vision.
- All policies on recruitment, evaluation, and firing are in line with EOE.
- Performance-based evaluation policies and procedures are in place and working.
- Policies on entitlement, compensation, and benefits are in place.
- Policies on drugs and alcohol and workplace violence are in place.

## Operations

Most organizations today, in their change and transformation process, are developing policies related to ending services and their related expenses. This often provides guidance to a key resource solution on the cost side, typically known as process redesign or reengineering. Technology often drives these efforts and demands policy review and formation. (See Chapter Six for more information on process redesign.)

For example, a service organization may hold as a value the maintenance of personal and high-touch relationships with its varied constituents. In order to implement this policy, the CEO and senior management may make a range of decisions concerning new technologies and office procedures. The organization may decide not to use automated messages and voice mail for incoming telephone calls. Instead, it maintains an individual whose sole purpose is to respond personally to each phone call, emphasizing the personal, caring nature of the organization. This policy may include the option of referring to an individual voice mail system. An example of a similar policy in action was implemented by Gateway Computers—a *Fortune* 500 company that employs a staff of about 150 people to answer all of their 800-number calls on the first ring.

Often you hear the CEO of an organization say, "I don't want my board in operations." Typically, CEOs expressing this feeling do not want unplanned and unmanaged interference in day-to-day activity. In the ideal situation, the board establishes the policy and helps develop the plans that direct the day-to-day activity of the organization, only becoming involved in operations when a particular board member's expertise and abilities can be of value to the organization and are specifically requested by the CEO and other managers.

### Financial Resources and Pricing

Policies related to seeking financial resources for underwriting the operations of an organization and building capital reserves for future service development are major agenda items for board leaders. Questions regarding financing, setting current ratios and business margins, tapping reserves for capital, developing in-service programs, and finding new donors are all policy questions.

Nonprofit boards need to ask, What enterprise or service areas deliver capital because they are profitable, while also fulfilling the organization's mission? Strong organizations today are asking and answering this question and are consequently making money. Of course, there is risk involved when new resource solutions are integrated into an organization's revenue mix and related policy issues must be addressed. Resource solutions must be constantly reviewed, based on research of current and potential target constituents. (See Chapter Six for more information on resource solutions.)

Policies related to the pricing of services are increasingly on the agenda of nonprofit organizations, even some social service organizations that have not traditionally dealt with pricing because of their low-income constituencies and policies related to mission. Pricing relates not only to the requirements of the budget but to the mission of the organization. A social service organization may decide to charge customers on a sliding scale, based on their ability to pay. In this way, some much-needed revenue may be generated without compromising the mission. Other organizations may establish policies that allow them to charge for some services but not for others.

Financial policies concerning mission and pricing may raise many questions that boards need to consider carefully. For example, is a college serving its mission to students who end up with a debt load that exceeds their repayment capacity? This is a serious policy issue many educational institutions need to address. As John Gehring (2000) pointed out in an on-line article, tuition rates rose faster in 2000 than the previous year's 2.6 percent inflation rate. In the fall of 2000, students at public institutions paid an average of 4.4 percent more for tuition than in 1999, whereas students at private universities paid 5 percent more.

How can a nonprofit organization establish pricing policies that will help meet the demands of those who can't pay for services, particularly if providing this service is part of the organization's mission? At what level does an organization cap uncompensated care and begin turning people away, even though its mission statement has historically focused on serving the underserved? An example is a church-related, long-term care organization in Texas that turns away Medicare patients when their reimbursement does not cover the cost of care, even though the institution's mission statement says it will serve all those in need. The board of this organization has undoubtedly struggled with this issue as it has established policies that reflect these actions. Sometimes a review and perhaps redrafting of an organization's mission statement is necessary.

Most nonprofit organizations today need to explore a variety of revenue-producing options beyond traditional dependence constituency support. For instance, organizations are looking at ways to partner or collaborate with other nonprofits, businesses, entrepreneurs, national associations, and international interests to attract resources to underwrite needed changes and developments for the organization. Insurance companies are courting health care organizations, and vice-versa. Colleges and universities are proposing collaboration with major corporations and businesses to provide contract education. Social service agencies are persuading governments to deliver new and innovative services at less cost and with more benefit to constituents. As all of these changes in funding sources are explored, related policies need to be continuously reviewed and frequently reformulated.

Philanthropy is becoming an increasingly essential source of revenue for all nonprofit organizations. Yet boards must actually make policy decisions to accept and seek gifts and grants. Particularly important is the question of what kinds of gifts and grants the organization is willing to accept, especially in the area of planned or estate gifts where property or other assets are given. After setting policy, many organizations find themselves rejecting gifts on an annual basis because the gift or grant requirements are out of step with the organization's policy or plans. Typically, this is an area where boards not only set the policy but are intensely involved in the implementation of fundraising efforts. (Chapter Six reviews philanthropy as a core responsibility of the nonprofit board.)

In summary, fully engaged boards need to be in constant touch with their policies as they relate to changes taking place in their organization. An organization's CEO also needs to play a crucial role in policy development by keeping the board informed of changes in operations or the marketplace as they affect policies. No new program or service should be established or eliminated without consideration of the policy implications. When an organization's mission changes, a complete review of policies as they reflect the mission is warranted. When a nonprofit's resource mix is altered, changes to related policies must also be considered.

Policy formation is an area of board responsibility that has remained a priority over the years. The engagement model of board governance being promoted in this book does not in any way suggest that boards should move away from their key responsibilities related to policy but asks that they add planning and marketing responsibilities to their plate of activities and that they include the CEO in the policy-planning process. Boards have always, first and foremost, been an organization's policy arbiters. If anything, that responsibility has intensified in these times of transformation when so much is changing and so much is at stake.

## Questions for Reflection

Has your board established appropriate policies in marketing, services, human resources, and financial resources?

Does your board continuously review established policies in light of rapidly changing environmental factors?

How does your board make appropriate policy decisions without becoming involved in day-to-day operations?

Does your board include the CEO in discussions about policies as they affect operations?

Do you feel uncomfortable bringing new issues or possible policy conflicts to the board for discussion and action?

How are your board and CEO recruitment efforts affected by policy considerations?

## Chapter Four

# Continuous Thinking
# and Planning

Plans are nothing. Planning is everything.
*Dwight D. Eisenhower*

In this chapter, board members will learn about the importance of being actively engaged in continuous thinking and planning in response to rapidly changing environments. They will recognize the need for board meetings to focus on substantive, interactive content discussion that leads to decision making.

Church leader Eugene chairs the board of a small midwestern college—an experience he has found to be personally fulfilling, particularly since the redesign of the board's planning process. In evaluating their performance as a board, Eugene and other board members expressed to the CEO a desire for a more flexible and consistent planning process—one that would be more engaging and would provide more opportunity for the college to adapt to a rapidly changing environment. The board endorsed the CEO's hiring of a consultant who worked in partnership with the chair, the planning committee, senior management, and a few selected leaders to develop a planning process for use well into the future. Board members went on a retreat with the goal of understanding and approving the process and connecting it to implementation. The organization has been successfully involved in continuous strategic thinking and planning since that retreat in 1994. Recent results show consistent increases in enrollment and margins, with a surplus budget moving money to reserves. In evaluations related to board performance and satisfaction, board members expressed excitement and genuine satisfaction about their board involvement.

Helen is a new board member of a cultural organization that has no planning process. She describes chaos and confusion about the mission of the organization. Each board meeting surprises her with new possible directions and financial crises; board members are asked to take action in a hurry to either cut or establish new programs. Her frustration is growing, and she wonders about continuing in an organization where decisions are reactionary rather than part of a plan. Helen continually asks herself if this board membership is a good use of her time. She wonders if she will have an opportunity to make a difference on this board. Yet she knows the other board members are talented and could have a tremendous impact on the organization if they were involved in the right kind of thinking, planning, and decision-making process.

Her challenge is this: How can she help take this board from its current unstructured milieu into a planning process and agenda that will allow substantive decisions to be based on the mission and resources of the organization—decisions that will stabilize the organization in the future? She embraces this challenge by presenting her concerns in great detail to the board and discovers that other board members have similar concerns. The board creates a committee to make recommendations for a new approach to planning that would involve an ongoing review of policy and mission. The result a year later is a board that is functioning in a much more organized and productive fashion and is able to respond effectively in its dynamic environment.

What did Eisenhower mean by the statement quoted at the beginning of this chapter? Eisenhower used planning as strategy formation and team building so that all the different countries participating under the umbrella of the allied forces were so prepared and so aligned in mission, vision, and strategy that their success was practically inevitable, even though many times they had to dramatically adjust their plans midstream. For instance, as D-Day approached, the weather was out of control and plans had to be delayed. The air force had to fly one hundred miles south of where it should have been. The resistance the allied forces encountered was much, much stronger than they had ever anticipated. As a result, the first leaders didn't make it through enemy lines. It was the fourth, fifth, and sixth lines of leadership that were taking small groups onto the beach and up the hill. The troops were so programmed and so oriented to their mission and vision of success that they won the day and achieved a turning-point victory for the allied forces.

Like Eisenhower, organizations facing ongoing change can anticipate challenging and difficult times, but they need to understand that plans must be adjusted as the environment changes. It may be the organization's third, fourth, or fifth level of staff that will need to adjust plans to fit the needs and desires of the customer. Therefore, team building is essential so that everyone throughout the organization understands the basic mission and vision, as defined by the organization's leadership. Eisenhower used this approach to planning to establish strategies and build a team that won the war.

## Setting the Stage for Continuous Planning

Continuous thinking and planning are at the heart of the engagement model of board governance and must take place at multiple levels throughout the organization. When change was more predictable and evolutionary, organizations took a great deal of time to plan. Perhaps once every several years, they developed a three- to five-year plan, possibly even a ten-year plan. Some organizations took up to two years or more to develop a strategic plan, based primarily on program audiences and budgets, that would be implemented in subsequent years. Human and financial resources, technology and facilities, services and markets—all were affected by this type of planning.

Times have changed. Peter Drucker in *Managing in a Time of Change* (1995) points out, "Uncertainty—in the economy, society, politics—has become so great as to render futile, if not counterproductive, the kind of planning most companies still practice: forecasting based on probabilities" (p. 39). This same uncertainty applies to nonprofit as well as for-profit organizations because they operate in similar environments.

Today, with fast-paced and unpredictable change taking place on an ongoing basis, boards operating in traditional planning modes often end up initiating strategies in one part of the organization while plans and programs are rapidly changing in another. Or by the time plans are implemented, they are already out of date. As a result, these organizations may not be operating efficiently or meeting their constituents' needs. Therefore, a new approach involving continuous thinking, analysis, and execution of plans is needed.

Continuous, responsive planning is a key component of our model for fully engaged boards in partnership with senior management. In the past, many nonprofit boards had plans presented to them by management, and their only role was to rubber-stamp these plans, sometimes after a superficial review. Today, fully engaged boards need to be actively involved in the thinking and reviewing of their organization's values, mission, vision, and design plan in order to become capable of sound decision making.

Many nonprofit boards are finding that they can only make accurate predictions about the environments in which their organizations will operate three to six months in advance. This means that boards need continual input from senior management so they can review financial projections, market and constituent attitudes, and perception shifts. Organizations may find that they need to regularly adjust their programming to provide the quality improvements demanded by customers who are sensitive to what is the "latest and the best."

As rapid transformation occurs in organizations and their markets, collaborative thinking needs to be taking place at the board level. Organizations can no longer operate in isolation. Rather, their leaders must collaborate with providers, vendors, and other market-related groups as they plan the development and the delivery of services. In order to be optimally effective, boards must be aware of the constantly emerging plans of related organizations.

Not all theorists believe boards should be involved in continuous planning, but the reality is that many boards are finding that their involvement in strategic thinking regarding markets, mission, vision, and values, in partnership with senior management, results in more flexible, productive planning that is responsive to changing markets.

An upper-midwestern college provides a good example of a board that has used a continuous planning process effectively and has been very successful while great changes were taking place in higher education. The college's president had been there for more than a decade and had served very well, but as the college's needs changed, so did its leadership needs. Growth had plateaued, and the board found that the organization was not capable of moving into an expansion mode and that quality issues were emerging. When board members elected to embark on a continuous planning process that was more responsive to environmental changes, they also realized they needed a dynamic leader with experience in change. The transition between leaders took place very positively, and a new leader assumed a leadership role in a flexible and collaborative planning process.

Continuous planning does not mean that plans should be completely spontaneous or that there is not also a place for more strategic long-term planning. There will always be a need for organizations to step back for more systemic study and analysis. All planning demands careful consideration and evaluation; however, boards that do not move quickly and take advantage of opportunities risk becoming obsolete in their marketplaces.

In another situation, a small community hospital board initiated a continuous planning process after marketplace research revealed great community concern about the small hospital being absorbed by a large system. The board partnered with the CEO to develop a strategy to remain independent. One of their key strategies was to develop a collaborative relationship with the larger system to bring more resources through partnerships into their community hospital. The hospital is still independent and is still continually monitoring its marketplace and reviewing its mission, plans, and policies as they relate to the community. The hospital's board continually monitors the dynamic health care environment in their community and is open to changes in their organization's plans if the need arises. This is an example of how a board of directors can use ongoing planning to be very effective in times of great change.

Boards that are in touch with their markets and react to changes with responsive plans usually become stronger, as do their organizations; board members are much more energized about their roles, and leadership is more effective. Nonprofit boards need to keep in mind the theme emphasized throughout this book: times are changing, organizations are transforming, and what might have worked ten years ago will not necessarily work now.

## Creating Structure for Rapid Response

Boards that embrace the concept of continuous planning create a structure and process for rapid response, allowing their organizations to respond to change in a timely fashion. In transforming organizations actively involved in continuous planning, the endings or beginnings of programs or initiatives can be more easily integrated into the organization's programming. In addition, the popular concept of continuous quality improvement ties in well with the continuous planning process. Board members involved in continuous planning become much more motivated and engaged, and new board members become active in organizations more quickly and easily.

Another approach that is enhanced by continuous planning is multiple scenarios planning—the ongoing examination of different paths toward accomplishing an objective. In changing organizations, there may be several ways to achieve growth and development goals. Board members should be responsible for identifying and choosing the scenarios that may be most effective. Boards need to evaluate possible scenarios carefully in light of financial resources and adherence to the organization's values and mission.

In the past, board members were frequently presented with a plan; they did not become actively involved in the development of options to consider. The result has been lack of board understanding, involvement, or commitment to the plan, creating a serious problem for any organization. Continuous thinking and planning open the door for multiple scenarios to be considered on an ongoing basis.

## Defining the Board's Role in Planning

The board's major responsibilities in the continuous collaborative planning process are to engage in strategic thinking, set policy related to emerging plans, review the capital needs of the plan, and provide assistance in planning for and accessing capital. It's important to emphasize that in a changing organization, these board tasks are pursued in partnership with the CEO and senior management. It is the CEO's responsibility to bring a process, budget, and eventually an operational plan to the board for review and endorsement.

It is also important to emphasize the importance of the individual human resources on the board as the plan emerges. The more diverse the representation on the board—the banker, the attorney, the investors, the constituent representative—the more effective board members will be in contributing to the planning process, in particular in helping access capital and in establishing relationships that will enhance the board's mission and goals.

## Reviewing Plan Components

At every board meeting, environmental issues and trends should be reviewed. And every review plan should cover an organization's external and internal markets. The external markets include the organization's chosen and potential markets; boards need to determine what the needs and opportunities are in these markets. In an era of rapidly changing markets, it is especially important to keep monitoring the marketplace. For instance, in the area of higher education for teachers, it would be important to talk to teachers regularly about their issues, their needs, the changes in their accreditation requirements, changes in the technologies they use, and changes in their students' needs. The institution educating these teachers needs to make sure that the learning options they need are being provided.

Internally, an organization needs to be constantly assessing its resources and its capabilities, based on marketplace information, and asking these questions: What areas of service need to be strengthened, changed, or even abandoned in light of changes in the marketplace? What resources and capabilities are available or need to be developed to support these changing plans?

For instance, in an environment such as health care, which is focused on constant quality improvement, it is essential to stay on top of changes in technology, treatments, and reimbursement as they affect patient care. Imagine where a health care organization would be if planning only took place every two or three years—or even every year. Successful health care organizations are continually evaluating and changing their plans in response to their rapidly transforming environment.

For years, Rotary International has maintained a highly successful worldwide polio immunization program with the goal of eradicating polio in the world. They are in the process of assessing the environment and determining what kind of program should be launched in the future because they have almost reached that goal.

A thorough environmental analysis will include all or most of the elements listed next. This information will provide a nonprofit organization with the informational tools needed to analyze the climate for its programs and services, as well as for resource development.

- Definition of geographic area or target market served, either by zip code, county, metropolitan statistical area, or state

- Demographic profile of the geographic area or target market served, including variables such as gender, age, income, educational level, total households, and other pertinent demographic data

- Psychographic profile of the geographic area or target market served, that is, a description of the primary lifestyle of those living within an organization's service area, including how people spend their time and money

- Projections for population growth or decline, by age, income, or other defined segment, for the geographic service area

- Demographic and psychographic profiles of those serviced by the organization—profiles of the "typical" client served by the organization, with separate profiles developed for each organization program, if appropriate

- Opinion research conducted among constituencies of the organization, including data on awareness and perceptions of the organization, communications effectiveness, and customer satisfaction

- A profile of the area business or economic climate, including total number of businesses, average business size, industry types, top twenty-five employers, gross product, and buying power

- A profile of the area's nonprofit climate, including the top twenty-five nonprofits, the top philanthropists or giving organizations, the three to five primary competing organizations, current campaigns within the area, and all federal funding programs for the area

- A profile of marketplace wants, desires, needs, and voids related to the community good

The familiar SWOT formula—Strengths, Weaknesses, Opportunities, Threats—provides a valuable tool for examining the environment in which an organization is operating. By looking closely at the strengths and weaknesses within an organization and at the opportunities and threats outside the organization, boards will have a clearer understanding of their planning needs.

Table 4.1 illustrates how a specific nonprofit board of directors used the SWOT formula to help them examine the environment affecting changes in their organization. After identifying these factors, this board was able to take advantage of their strengths and opportunities while addressing ways to improve in their areas of weakness and deal with the threats to their organization.

A SWOT analysis can help nonprofit organizations ask the right questions before implementing strategies. The process can be intensive and does not encompass the entire planning process, but success at this level will later enable the planning team to formu-

#### Table 4.1. SWOT Analysis of Leadership

| Strengths | Weaknesses |
|---|---|
| Strong leadership emerging at important decision point for mission | Lack of internal leadership development strategies |
| Enterprise healthy and growing | Current organizational structure and compensation models complicating and limiting leadership options |
| Vision beginning to build momentum | |
| Innovative, member-focused programs developing throughout enterprise | Internal silos limiting strategic vision and understanding in middle management |
| | Cynicism about corporate policies |

| Opportunities | Threats |
|---|---|
| Recruitment of senior executives from outside the organization | Leadership succession reflecting compromise rather than decisiveness |
| Synergy of initiatives transforming organization | Political fights becoming disruptive |
| Direction of transformed organization emphasizing mission and member focus | Rapid change in environment requiring decisions beyond abilities of new leadership to repond |
| | Potential emergence of nonmission-oriented senior leadership |

late appropriate strategies, tactics, and action plans to address the selected issues.

For instance, a SWOT analysis conducted at a small, religious midwestern college that was floundering identified some significant external opportunities in the marketplace for growth, including an intense interest in lifelong learning, a huge demand for teachers, and a growing parental desire for religious education. External threats to the university included the media distilling moral values, the rising costs of tuition, and the increasing amount of competition from peer institutions. Internal strengths were also identified, including a high-quality teaching faculty and a proven track record of excellence. Weaknesses were also examined, such as an unwillingness to take risks and a campus that was not visitor-friendly. Many more factors were identified in this SWOT survey; however, the basic findings were extremely helpful and provided a framework for the planning process.

### Marketplace Position

An organization's position in its marketplace is where customers or constituents see the organization in relation to competition. Many nonprofit organizations have no idea how their customers perceive the organization; they base plans and policies on the board's perception of the organization's position. Boards need accurate, timely information, perhaps through satisfaction surveys, about their organization's marketplace position. In volatile, changing markets, this kind of crucial information needs to be constantly solicited and updated. Plans and policies need to be based on the most current information possible (see Chapter Five.)

### Assumptions

Assumptions are ideas that are tested in the form of qualitative research related to the current market base and the organization's capabilities for serving that market. In many successful organizations, assumptions are verified through good research analysis and information reviews.

For example, a common assumption in health care is that costs will continue to rise while traditional sources of revenue, such as government funding and insurance, will continue to tighten. The obvious implication is that health care organizations must find other ways to ensure that their costs are covered, particularly in light of a nonprofit's mission of ensuring health care access across all economic levels. This assumption must be continually tested and verified; in some cases, hospitals may face the difficult dilemma of reconsidering their missions.

Another health care example involves the much-tested assumption that cigarette smoking is a core cause of lung cancer and other serious health care problems, inevitably leading to increased health care costs. This assumption leads to the conclusion that if we can find ways to reduce smoking in America, we can reduce the cost of health care. The question, then, for a community hospital board that is responsible for the public trust is, What can the organization do in the way of preventive measures to reduce smoking? The answer to this question could become a major board initiative in a continuous planning process.

### Mission, Values, and Vision

Every organization's plans should go back to the mission, values, and vision of the organization, particularly as these elements change during transformation. Boards of directors should continually be reviewing values and plans based on their support of the mission.

The definitions in the sections to follow may be helpful in determining whether an organization has adequately defined and developed these important elements.

**Mission.**   The *mission* of an organization is the fundamental purpose for its existence—its reason for being. A mission statement answers the "why" question related to an organization's purpose.

In *The Mission Statement Book* (1995), Abrahams refers to the Trinova Corporation's definition of mission, which says, in part: "A mission statement is an enduring statement of purpose for an organization that identifies the scope of its operations in product and market terms, and reflects its values and priorities" (p. 38).

This is an appropriate definition of mission for either a for-profit or nonprofit organization; however, you will find major differences in the underlying values reflected in the mission statements of for-profit and noprofit organizations.

An example of a nonprofit mission statement (in this case a social service agency) is, "To support and improve the emotional, mental, and physical development of residents in a particular central city community, helping them become more self-sufficient and lead more satisfying lives."

**Values.** *Values* are the essential beliefs of the organization, particularly those that serve to distinguish it from similar entities. Core values are the principles that shape and form an institution at its deepest level. They define the charter of the organization and are intrinsic to the purpose of the organization.

Organizations rarely sit back and say, What is the value of our organization in our community? They may look at their values as an organization, but they don't look at what the customer and community leaders might say about the organization's value. The answer to this question may raise some important issues, especially when an organization sees its customer base weakening. How the community perceives the organization's value is a component of market position.

Values for the social service agency mentioned earlier might be such concepts as "the basic value of each and every human life" and "the importance of self-esteem and self-responsibility in living a full life."

**Vision.** *Vision* is the direction the organization is going, based on its mission and values. Vision is usually expressed in an inspirational and compelling statement that describes a desired future reality the organization is striving to achieve.

A vision engages people—reaching out and grabbing them in the gut. It is tangible, energizing, highly focused. People get it right away; it takes little or no explanation. It requires no more than one sentence to say. It is a "we" statement because it reflects a collective vision. It is not dependent on a specific leader to carry out. It is in sync with the organization's mission and values.

The social service agency's vision might be, "We strive to bring excellence in health care to every person in the community" or "We will provide preschool education to every child in the community."

In times of transformation, it is likely that an organization's values will change; mission and vision statements will inevitably need to change, too. When these fundamental changes take place, boards must go back to the drawing board with their policies and plans. If this does not happen, it is possible that with so many external changes evolving so quickly, a board may suddenly find itself planning programs that do not reflect their organization's mission. A continual referral to mission and values, as they affect plans, is essential in a changing environment.

### Financial Models

An integral part of planning is structuring the financial component of the plan based on projected resources. It is surprising how many nonprofit boards have no idea about the financial variables affecting their organizations. They may see a budget but have no explanation or understanding of the assumptions on which the budget is based. They may make significant programming or service decisions without considering their financial implications, except on a superficial level. How can a board of directors make sound financial decisions when there is no real comprehension of the impact of their decisions or the related variables involved?

For example, the CEO of an art museum presented the board of directors with a proposal for a major program expansion on two fronts: adding a new, large gallery for traveling shows and expanding an educational program for underprivileged children in the community. After reviewing these plans, the board was initially receptive; however, they needed to answer this key question: How could the organization finance these projects?

A board committee, headed by a corporate financial officer who was a board member and including the CEO, was formed to explore the financial viability of both ventures and then present its recommendations to the board. Their resulting report revealed that the revenue projected from increased attendance at traveling shows, based on research the committee conducted into the experiences of other museums, would more than cover the cost of the physical expansion and also the increased educational programming. In addition, the board determined that the new educational program could be partially underwritten by corporate sponsors who committed before the projects were launched. The projected result was increased revenue for the museum in addition to sufficient financing for both projects.

These projections were very carefully fine-tuned and reviewed by the organization's outside accountants, who recommended that the board approve the project. Throughout the development process, the CEO continually monitored expense and revenue projects and made regular reports to the board. In one instance, the board directed that changes be made in the building expansion project to accommodate increasing costs. Two years later, the projected revenue has materialized; of course, the CEO is being praised for his foresight in planning, and the board is being praised for its diligent financial oversight role. This is an ideal example, reflecting the engagement model, of how a board and CEO can work together to achieve a major goal for their organization.

In another situation, a university board of directors was trying to evaluate its tuition structure as a rate increase was being considered.

Yet many complex variables were involved that took a deep understanding of the financial implications. The questions that needed to be answered before a decision could be made were complicated and far-reaching:

What are the assumptions concerning investments and endowments?

What are the program and scholarship costs?

What new programs are being planned?

How much will faculty compensation increase?

How will inflation (or deflation) affect the cost of living in the next year?

How much is tuition already discounted?

What projections can be made about revenue sources?

Other considerations involved student capacity for handling a tuition increase and the competitive position of the university in its marketplace. A board committee and the CEO, working with a financial consultant, took on the task of answering these questions and creating a financial model that could be presented and explained to the board in great detail. Related issues were explored, and a report was developed on those issues. A one-day retreat was organized around the financial implications of the tuition increase. The board ultimately decided to raise the tuition to an appropriate amount that would cover increased expenses—a step that the board felt students could handle and that placed the university in an acceptable position competitively.

A board of directors must have financial models developed, presented, and fully explained by the organization's CEO or CFO or an outside financial professional before any informed decisions can be made. The board can then return again and again to this financial model as plans and decisions are being made to determine how they fit the model. Sometimes the model must be changed. In a time of transformation, most financial models are in a continual state of review and adjustment.

## Evaluation of Current Plan Success

Every board meeting should include some aspect of plan review on its agenda. When this review process reveals that aspects of the current plan need redirection, steps to make that happen should be identified and implemented. In this way, the plan is under a constant state of evaluation and renewal.

## Choosing a Continuous Planning Model

The illustration of a model for planning (see Figure 4.1) represents a continuous and interactive planning process, which is key to the engagement model for board governance. The arrows suggest that plan elements interact with one another and are interdependent. This model emphasizes the need for ongoing reflection and interactive communication concerning the elements of the model.

**Figure 4.1. Continuous Planning Model**

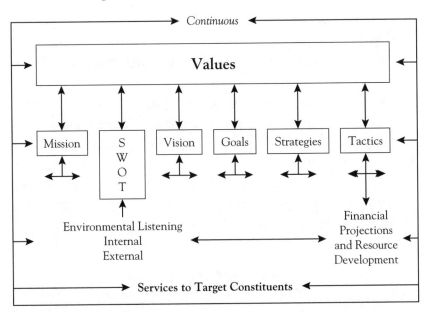

In a transforming environment, boards should always be connected to the marketplace through listening, analyzing, and responding. To be responsive, boards constantly need to manage and adjust human and financial resources, processes, and systems. This model is based on assumptions that a board's planning process should do the following:

- Adjust quickly to the environment
- Be continuous
- Integrate stakeholders, experts, customers, constituent leaders, and partners
- Be action-oriented
- Include mechanisms for implementation, management, and accountability
- Include a way to evaluate plan results
- Include the CEO and policymakers
- Include strategy making and strategy programming
- Include a communication process
- Keep it simple
- Connect clearly to the budgeting and staffing process

Boards need to constantly look at all these elements as part of their planning process. As plan tactics or actions are implemented, the results can be very instructive. If the tactics succeed, the board knows it can continue to move forward as planned. If they fail, adjustments may be needed in strategies and goals. In a continuous planning situation, good information leads to ongoing adjustment of plans, services, human resources, systems, and financial projections.

## Using a Variety of Tools

A variety of tools and resources can be helpful in the continuous planning process, including customer satisfaction surveys, newmarket analyses, independent quality evaluations, and informal strategic focus groups.

In addition, a variety of other activities will enhance the continuous planning process. Interactive communication among board members, management, related organizations, constituents, and other market groups will result in a heightened involvement, improved feedback, and a valuable sense of ownership among all parties. Boards should also focus on the development of channels that connect constituents in the thinking and planning process.

These channels can actively involve constituents and might include

- Ad hoc committees or task groups organized around specific projects
- Web site forums
- Reports and newsletters on customer feedback related to the quality or improvement of work
- Gatherings of target groups (for example, alumni, patient families, faculty) to discuss projects and give value to the planning process

As an example, an organization serving developmentally disabled individuals (mentioned in Chapter Two) reorganized their board as the result of a self-assessment. Subsequently, they undertook a planning process as they realized the need for continuous planning and thinking in the face of a rapidly changing field. Recent years had seen significant social and demographic trends that had an impact on the environment in which the organization delivered service. Huge shifts in funding sources and a diminishing labor force, among other issues, presented new challenges to the board of directors.

For the first time in this organization's history, the board integrated market research and constituent listening as key components in their planning process. They started by conducting interviews and focus groups among key constituent groups, including volunteer leadership, direct care staff, and parents and guardians of clients. They also conducted a written survey of all employees throughout the United States, something that had never before been done. The board used findings from this listening process to refine mission and vision statements and to define six strategic directions for the future of the organization. Mission, vision, and these new directions were then tested in a two-day facilitated retreat that brought almost one hundred people together, including administrative and direct care staff, board members and major donors, families and clients. The highlight of the meeting was a panel discussion among the organization's clients, which underscored the new direction of listening and responding to the needs of constituents.

The board emerged from this planning process with a new sense of direction for the organization, a shared vision and purpose, and a renewed sense that they were doing truly important work for their clients and their communities around the country.

## Organizing Action Teams

Self-directed action teams can be very effective in taking plans to the action stage. In an engagement model, these teams consist of leaders and others within the organization at all levels, including board members and representatives of senior management, as well as people from outside the organization and from capital sources. These leaders should be enlisted because of their expertise, innovative thinking, interest in the task at hand, and overall leadership qualities. Action teams are typically integrated across the system and are asked to develop tactics or action steps to accomplish strategies. They need to be empowered with decision-making capabilities and the resources to develop a plan and implement action. The actions of these teams can be checked continually against the organization's vision, mission, values, and goals.

Action teams can be a pivotal part of the planning process, developing tactics and identifying the resource requirements necessary to achieve core planning goals and strategies. Action teams can be formed around broad goals, with subteams forming as necessary. Frequently, action teams are cochaired by internal and external leaders, under whose direction the team is asked to provide leadership in the following ways:

- Review goals and strategies developed by the board
- Conduct (or request) further research necessary to support the development of tactics
- Develop tactics to meet goals and strategies
- Identify the human and financial resource requirements needed to fully implement strategies
- Identify evaluation methods to be used and constituent benefits from goal attainment
- Package recommendations for board review

As an example, a social service agency board decided that in order to respond to changing needs in the marketplace, the organization needed a much more flexible workforce of both internal and external knowledge workers. The board created a self-directed action team, which was assigned the responsibility of putting together a comprehensive plan for this human resources shift while considering all the implications for the organization, from impact on its financial model to its public relations position.

This team developed a plan that effectively addressed many complex issues, including how to recruit new workers, how to shift positions of current workers, how to compensate and evaluate contract workers, and how to develop contracts. They established a timeline for making this significant shift from an all-employee workforce to a combination employee-contractor workforce. Members of the action team represented every department in the organization, along with a board member and representatives from management. The result was a very smooth and successful transition that was understood and accepted by the entire organization.

Action teams can provide an especially meaningful venue for board members or prospective board members to become involved in the organization. For example, at a small university, a board member who had indicated interest in technology was asked to serve on an action team exploring how the university could provide technological expertise for businesses and industry in the community. When the team ultimately decided to plan a technology and communications center, this board member was so excited about the project that she brought her own significant resources to the table to help underwrite the building to house the new center. The board was wise to include this board member on the action team, not only because of her philanthropy but because she lent her deep interest and contagious enthusiasm to the project and provided an effective liaison with the board. The action team gave her a venue for using her considerable talents to benefit the organization. The action team approach was also an ideal way for the board to maintain close involvement with the project and for the organization to move forward on this project in an efficient and productive manner.

## Involving Board, Management, and Others in Planning

The continuous planning process should be led by the board of directors in conjunction with the CEO and senior management, who need to be involved at all levels in overseeing the planning process and integrating changes as the organization is transformed. Other valuable support may be solicited from specialized organization staff members, outside experts and consultants, constituent leaders (the customers), and major donors and representatives of other sources of capital. In the past, many organizations assigned planning to the CEO with the possible assistance of selected key managers and board members; however, in today's dynamic environment, bringing together a broader group of people and involving an entire board will result in stronger, more effective planning.

The process of effective continuous planning will almost always result in a stronger board because it develops the kind of leadership that meets overall objectives despite variations in the implementation process. As a result of continuous planning, many boards see a strengthening of leadership at all levels, starting with the board itself and then moving into management. An atmosphere for developing and strengthening leadership both inside and outside the organization is created when ideas are discussed, appropriate business scenarios are selected, and meaningful interaction takes place between the board and management.

## Planning to Keep Planning

In a climate of transformation, planning is never complete. Does that mean that boards do nothing but plan? No. Boards have other important activities, as discussed throughout this book; however, it is through participation in effective planning that board members provide strong leadership. Participation in creating visions and strategies at the appropriate level is a key board responsibility that builds a strong foundation for an organization's development and growth. Implementation and evaluation of plans is also essential to creating and maintaining successful organizations.

The buzz phrase a decade or more ago was *strategic planning*—a concept that means different things to different people. Generally, however, the term separated thinking from implementation and was viewed as the optimum approach to developing successful organizations. Now the term suggests status quo reprogramming that is based on an organization's current direction rather than on a dynamic vision of the future. Managers are discovering that strategic planning, as it was defined historically, may be too static and tedious. In a changing environment, boards need to focus on continuous thinking about the future, followed by tactical and operational planning, which leads directly to implementation.

In the engagement model of board leadership, boards set up a continuous planning process that doesn't necessarily take place within a defined period of time as the traditional strategic planning approach does. Within this continuous planning process there may be a lot of strategic or operational thinking going on. As an example, a college in Nebraska is actually in its third cycle of continuous planning—a process that began in the early 1990s. Each cycle is built on the last and has engaged the board and the college leadership in strategic thinking around organizational values, mission, and vision as they relate to decision making and to changes in programs and services. As the result of this thinking, the college president has developed operational plans and strategies that have carried the college forward during a decade of change. A board member sat on a planning coordinating team as a way of connecting the planning process more closely to the board. Consequently, the board was involved in planning every step of the way.

So many times, boards start to develop plans before they have gathered information, assessed the marketplace, and gone through the essential thinking process. The most important point here is that thinking should take place before developing strategy and before the development of operational and action plans. The board's key role in making changes is to do the necessary thinking with the CEO and senior management that will lead to the strategic or operational plans that then become the driving force for implementation.

In order to provide direction for planning, board members and senior managers may want to team with outside experts and customers to think about the changes that will take place in the future—and perhaps the very near future. Key questions can direct this thinking process:

> What changes will take place in the organization's marketplace, capabilities, and ability to attract resources?
>
> How will the organization's mission and vision change, and what values will need to be revised?

Once changes have been projected, leaders throughout an organization need to engage in the kind of deep thinking and research that can effectively direct the continuous planning process. These leaders, in partnership with the CEO, core management, and talent within the organization, need to develop the tactics and resources necessary to put plans into operation and then direct the implementation process and the evaluation of results.

Listening to an organization's constituency was a key ingredient in a successful strategic plan that dramatically increased philanthropy at the Caron Foundation, one of the country's oldest and largest addiction treatment centers located in Pennsylvania. In the mid-1990s, when a new CEO was hired, ten carefully facilitated planning sessions were conducted so that the new CEO and board could "listen" to their constituency. Also, interviews were held by phone and input was requested via a newsletter. After the input was processed and the strategic plan launched, this organization doubled its revenue and increased its philanthropy by 600 percent over five years.

A word of caution: Boards of nonprofit organizations need to apply their expertise to thinking and planning on a broad level. Then, as decisions are made about corporate direction, management should have the responsibility of developing operational and implementation plans to bring back to their boards for review. Certainly, it could be valuable to tap into a board member's specific area of expertise as operational planning occurs, but it's really the role of the CEO to develop the response to overall strategic plans.

## Moving Away from Traditional Planning

Organizations moving from a traditional planning model to a continuous model need to understand what they have been doing and why it's important to do something different. Their board members should think about a continuous model design that fits their organization and the environment in which they're operating.

It may not be easy for boards to break out of their old planning patterns. Sometimes boards and CEOs spend major amounts of time on planning, but they never get to the action stage for two main reasons: (1) the financial or staffing resources (or both) aren't there, or (2) they never get to the point of identifying the steps to be taken, and, if they do get to this point, they never actually empower people to take those steps. Organizations can break out of their ineffective planning patterns by creating a structure that will act. This can be accomplished through careful structuring of a new continuous planning process that balances thinking, making decisions, and empowering people to take action.

Bringing people who will take action into the planning process will help make this happen. Boards need to focus on planning that is connected to implementation because the continuous planning process is grounded in team work. The board does its part by thinking, forming policies, and approving plans. The CEO partners with the board and develops operational and implementation plans; action team members from the organization who will implement the plan should be involved throughout the process.

---

### Questions for Reflection

Why do boards in changing organizations need to shift from five-year strategic plan models to continuous planning models? Does this need to happen in your organization?

How long has it been since your board has reviewed its mission and vision, as well as its underlying values?

Do you suspect that your board needs to know more about environmental issues affecting your institution?

How will this shift to continuous planning be accomplished on your board?

What roles should your board members, CEO, and staff play in the planning process?

What are some of the most effective ways to evaluate how your plans are being implemented?

*Chapter Five*

# Positioning and Public Relations

The advent of the Internet is making it more
common for people to be able to manage many
more relationships than in the past; however, they
are valuing fewer, deeper relationships for personal
(face-to-face) involvement.

*Gary J. Hubbell*

In this chapter, board members will understand the importance of
identifying and targeting their organization's position and key relationships in priority markets, and will recognize their essential role
in establishing important external relationships.

Mark is a senior executive in a major corporation in his community.
He was asked by a local liberal arts university to sit on its board of directors primarily because of his connections in the business community. The board anticipated expanding the university's business
school and adding an MBA program in the near future, knowing it
needed expertise and help on the board to attract students, develop
business support, and raise funds. Mark understands the board's expectations clearly and has become actively involved in soliciting the
backing of area businesses for the school's new business program. He
was appointed to head a task force, including other board members,
senior management, and faculty, thus spearheading the marketing of
the business school expansion. In this role, he guided the organization to target a new market of potential students among the young

business professionals in the community. Other board members have learned much from Mark's approach to marketing and have also started to develop important community relationships beneficial to the university. The business community's perception of the university as a valuable community asset has been significantly enhanced since the expansion project was launched. The business school expansion has been a very successful venture for the university, in great part because of the board's close involvement under Mark's leadership.

When Helen was being considered as a prospective member of a major nonprofit health care system board of directors, there was some hesitation among current board members because of her lack of direct business experience. However, she was ultimately asked to join the board because she was an articulate and talented leader in the community being served by the system. She was also an active volunteer in a variety of other nonprofits serving the same market with different services. Because of her vast networking capacity, she has been able to help the organization on many fronts, bringing in new groups of donors, initiating some exciting collaborative relationships that have expanded the system's customer base, and identifying developing market needs that have inspired significant new programming for the system. The board president often observes that because of her enthusiasm, commitment, and wide range of relationships, she may be the most effective person who has ever served on the board. Boards need people like Helen, whose expertise is in developing relationships.

The engagement model for board members highlights positioning the organization and developing relationships as key board functions. The importance of these functions cannot be emphasized enough. Every aspect of an organization's operations is affected by its position in the market, from setting policy and planning to raising funds, pricing, and evaluating results. Positioning starts in the consumer's mind. It is not just what the consumer thinks of an organization but how an organization compares to other institutions in the mind of the consumer.

Ries and Trout (*Positioning: The Battle for Your Mind*, 2001) introduce the concept of positioning in a clear manner: "Positioning is not what you do to a product. Positioning is what you do to the mind of the prospect. That is, you position the product in the mind of the prospect" (p. 2). Ries and Trout go on to say, "Positioning is an organized system for finding a window in the mind. It is based on the concept that communication can only take place at the right time and under the right circumstances" (p. 19).

In a time of change, it is particularly important for a board to be continually monitoring its position in the eyes of its constituents because position can change dramatically as the environment changes. Sometimes these changes take place almost overnight, so a very first step in establishing position is determining what is in the constituent's mind. The questions must be asked: How do your customers (both current and prospective) perceive the similarities and differences among your organization's services and products? and What attributes of these services do they consider most valuable in their buying decisions?

A major way an organization can achieve its desired position in the community is through the development of relationships. As an organization targets its priority markets for service, resources, and benefits to customers, board members have a crucial role in building the relationships that will help position the organization within these markets. Board members need to help identify, introduce, and cultivate these vital relationships.

An example of a nonprofit board of directors that realized the importance of building relationships in the community was the board of a social service agency with a mission to feed the hungry. The board had members who had been with the organization from its beginning twenty years ago, as well as representatives from the food industry in which it operated. A very strong entrepreneurial executive director led the organization and worked closely with its board of directors.

The board became highly engaged in building relationships within the community and profiling the right community leaders to test planning initiatives. The board members also played diverse roles in advancing their capital campaign. Early founders were intensely involved in building and managing relationships. Others were exceptionally good at the operational side, ensuring a sound business plan; still others were focused on getting the endorsement of leaders in the food industry. Thus board leaders had strengths in

- Telling the long story of the organization
- Pointing to business benefits
- Getting the endorsements of the "right" people

They all played a strategic role in building awareness of the organization in the community, where its benefits had been a well-kept secret. Board members were successful in holding meetings over luncheons to bring in potential supporters. This relationship-building activity led to

- Clarification of the board's roles
- Greater board involvement in the organization
- A more strategic partnership with the executive director
- Strategic recruitment of key business people
- The donation of $1 million from a businessperson who appreciated the organization's business model and joined the board of directors

## Focusing on Public Relations

Once a board has identified its preferred market, the board, in partnership with the CEO, should be continually looking for market leaders and opinion makers who can be introduced to the organization through events, programs, publications, media coverage, and services. These leaders can be a tremendous source of feedback in terms of the marketplace, but they can also assist in the positioning process if they start to develop significant relationships with the organization.

As an example, a very committed board member of a large alcohol and drug treatment organization held regular coffees in his home for different leaders in the community. During these coffees, he would discuss the related issues of alcohol abuse, employment, and quality of life in the community, emphasizing the programming of his organization that was effectively addressing these issues. Many benefits to the organization were generated by this board member's efforts. New friends were developed for the organization; people with similar concerns were discovered; the word spread throughout the community about the good work going on in the organization; candidates for board membership and philanthropy were identified; and the position of the organization in the eyes of the community was greatly enhanced. This example reflects grassroots public relations at its best.

## Emphasizing "Brand" Identity

Another key concept related to positioning that is emphasized today in businesses and more recently in nonprofit organizations is "brand," which refers to the values the consumer associates with an organization. Brand identity gets at the core values of the marketplace in relation to an organization. For example, when one thinks of Volvo, the immediate brand identity is "safety"; for Maytag it's "reliability." In a hospital it might be "cutting-edge technology," or in a social service agency it might be "customer service" or "commitment to the underserved."

It is a key board responsibility to guide the organization in identifying its desired brand identity. It is especially important while an organization and its environment are going through change for boards to stay in close touch with the values that reflect this brand identity. Organizations don't want the changes taking place to veer away from their constituents' values. Even with the most radical transformation, organizations need to make sure they are always reflecting the brand identity that's been targeted. And customers' core values may be changing, too; that needs to be understood as programs are designed.

Boards should consider embarking on brand studies through which they may be able to retrieve a great deal of in-depth information in a short period of time. Brand studies may consist of one-on-one interviews or may take the form of small constituent focus groups, where people are interviewed at length about their perceptions of an organization. This approach allows boards to see the complete picture that constituents have of their organization and also opens the door to new issues they might not have considered. In a climate of rapid change, a brand study can be especially helpful because it gives constituents the opportunity to bring up new ideas, and there is an immediacy to the process. A side benefit is that by keeping key constituents involved, relationships are being developed and maintained as organizations are going through potentially disruptive transitions.

For example, the board of directors of a very large nonprofit organization decided, as they prepared for a transformation process, that they wanted to test their position in their preferred marketplace. They did this through both quantitative and qualitative research in the form of a brand study. Their study, which consisted of about two hundred interviews with constituents, revealed that a high percentage of their marketplace perceived them as being highly committed to Christian values and very competent in their field. But it also revealed that the constituents wanted to feel more connected to their organization. This information was extremely helpful as the organization planned its transformation. The board knew they needed to keep emphasizing their values and quality, but they also needed to establish strong programs that carried their mission into the community. The process of conducting the brand study was itself an initial step in building relationships and establishing more connections to the marketplace.

## Researching Your Market

As part of a continuous planning process, boards need to identify market niches and segments within their organization's constituent groups. Board members are in a unique position to communicate with the leaders and opinion makers within these groups. It is appropriate that board members are frequently asked to serve on boards because they represent one or more of these groups and because they are respected peers of other leaders in these market segments.

Board members who are poised to assist in the positioning process need to have a deep understanding of the mission, vision, and values of the organization they represent. As explained in the previous chapter, in the continuous planning model board members and the CEO need to continually review and discuss these key plan components. An advantage of continuous planning is that it prepares involved board members to accurately (and perhaps passionately) articulate the organization to market leaders.

It is also important for board members to know the history of relationships with priority markets. This question needs to be answered: How is the organization currently serving the market, and what satisfaction indicators point to successful service or perhaps inadequate service to its markets? Board members and the CEO must review this information regularly in order to fulfill a number of roles, as well as the role of positioning. Qualitative research through focus groups, as described earlier in the section on brand studies, can be a very effective and quick way to generate this information.

Focusing on the following issues and questions may be helpful in identifying and organizing the information boards need in order to evaluate their positions within their markets. Understanding your customers is, of course, the first step in market positioning. (See Chapter Four for helpful information on identifying a customer base.)

### Constituent Needs

What needs or desires can the organization fill for its constituents?

How well do constituents think the organization is meeting those needs?

How satisfied are constituents with the products and services provided by the organization?

### Perceived Value

What value would constituents say they receive from the organization's products and services?

What value would constituents say they receive from being connected with the organization?

What would constituents be willing to pay for the value they receive from the organization's products and services? (This may not be applicable to some nonprofits where constituents do not pay for services.)

### Constituent Behaviors

How frequently do constituents purchase products or services or make donations to the organization?

How recently have constituents purchased products or services or made a donation to the organization?

What is the average size of purchases or donations?

Do constituents intend to purchase or donate in the future?

In what circumstances do constituents typically purchase or donate?

The answers to all these questions, as well as their implications, need to be understood as a whole by the board in order to make effective decisions about the organization's direction.

Too often, nonprofit organizations rely on their own internal viewpoint or a few anecdotal voices to answer these questions rather than take the time to listen qualitatively and quantitatively to their constituents. Or they focus all of their research efforts on customer satisfaction surveys, without connecting their products or services to primary constituent needs. It is possible for a customer to be extremely satisfied with a product or service and to express this on a satisfaction survey but to have no intention of ever purchasing it again because their needs have changed. By seeing a broad picture of constituent needs, values, and behaviors, an organization can better understand the role it plays in their constituents' lives and anticipate what that relationship should be in the future.

Nonprofits also need to understand what kinds of relationships their constituents are seeking. The organization can then develop an approach to constituent relationship building that satisfies this constituent need, being careful not to lump all constituents in a market into one group. Each person should be treated as an individual with unique needs. Some constituents may be seeking a heavy user relationship; others might be looking for occasional or part-time use. Then there might be supporters who reap different kinds of benefits from their involvement—a feeling of benevolence, recognition, or networking opportunities. The main point is that it is absolutely essential to know exactly what each constituent segment wants out of the relationship.

It may be helpful to think of constituents as fish in a pond, influenced by the many currents and events around them, as well as other inhabitants of the pond. Every time an organization conducts an event, contacts donors, publishes a newsletter, or is covered in the local papers, those events "wash over" constituents. However, the way throwing a rock in a pond produces ever-widening circles of waves, the information has usually become diffused by the time it reaches constituents.

At the same time, other organizations are sending their own messages or "rocks" into the pond, and the waves of information are changing as they intersect. Likewise, an organization's constituents are being influenced by their peer groups, for instance, the other inhabitants of the pond, who have their own perceptions of the organization and are likely to share their perceptions with the organization's constituents. It is critical for nonprofit boards to understand how all of these influences, most of which are beyond the board's direct control, combine and are understood by constituents.

Determining these important points will undoubtedly involve some careful investigation. Although corporate America has been involved in such vital market research for a long time, very few nonprofit organizations understand the necessity for doing this kind of research. Nonprofits need to become much more customer-focused in order to compete in an increasingly competitive and demanding environment. Before board members start cultivating relationships, they need to understand where their organization is currently positioned in the marketplace and what their positioning goals are for the future.

## Understanding Your Competitors

It is very important for board members to understand how their organization is perceived, compared to its competitors. This is just as important as understanding how constituents are directly related to the organization. Keep in mind that constituents are being bombarded with many different messages from many different angles. The information one group is sending may not be received in exactly the way intended because of other information being received.

Key questions need to be asked in relation to an organization's identified competition:

How is the organization distinguished from competitors in the mind of the consumer?

Is this the way the board wants the organization to be distinguished?

If not, what can the board and management do to change this perception?

If so, what can they do to maintain and build on this perception?

For example, the board of directors of a group of small, private Christian colleges conducted research revealing that fewer than 6 percent of their denomination's seniors were choosing their colleges. This finding led them to a brand study to determine what would encourage these students to choose this group of colleges over other colleges and universities. The board discovered that their brand identity was very vague among high school juniors, seniors, and guidance counselors, whereas their competitors were making their identities very clear. There was much more name recognition among their competitors.

This information led the board to establish an intense program to build their colleges' brand identity in their market. Another study helped them identify the values that were important to their market of prospective students—values of excellence in education, combined with deep religious commitment. The board then launched a positioning and public relations campaign to associate these values with their institutions. This comprehensive marketing campaign over the next several years was tremendously successful and resulted in significantly increasing their numbers of well-qualified applicants over the next five years.

When planning positioning efforts in relation to competitors, it's important to realize that every organization not only has specific competitors—the organizations that provide similar services—but generic competitors. Generic competitors include all the ways a customer can spend resources other than by relating to a specific organization. For instance, higher education might say that one of its prime generic competitors is employment, which some potential students choose, at least for a time, over education. Or a church on Sunday morning may have a major generic competitor in the form of the national football league's pregame shows on TV.

A final word of caution about competition: Although it's important for boards to be aware of competition, they should not become obsessed with it, allowing this concern to distract them from their primary goals. A board's major positioning focus needs to be on creating and communicating the distinctive image that they want to have associated with their organization. In many instances, competitors in a marketplace should be viewed positively because they generate interest in an organization's area of service. A board can define its organization's own niche in the marketplace, and competitors can have theirs. It's impossible for any organization to be everything to everyone.

## Targeting Relationships Within Priority Markets

With the help of board members (or their contacts) who represent each market or subgroup within a market, lists can be developed of leaders in each group. These lists need to be carefully reviewed by board members, and relationship targets should be identified based on the target's influence within their group and on the board's resources for establishing relationships.

For example, a national or international religious organization might choose leaders from foundations or companies where board members have connections as contacts for building relationships and positioning resources. If the organization has no board members with appropriate contacts for these targeted relationships, then some key questions need to be asked, such as, Is this really a priority market for customers and resources? And if so, should the organization target this market in selecting board members?

It is important to remember that most identifiable markets have leaders who influence others within that market and who have established regular lines of communication within that market. These are the leaders who need to be identified because they have the potential for sending powerful, positive messages about an organization within that market.

The "market tree" in Figure 5.1 reflects the wide scope of relationships that a social ministry organization needed to consider when identifying its key relationships in the market.

Significant constituents to consider are divided into three key groups: (1) *users*, who may also be viewed as customers or those

## Figure 5.1. Market Tree of Constituent Segments

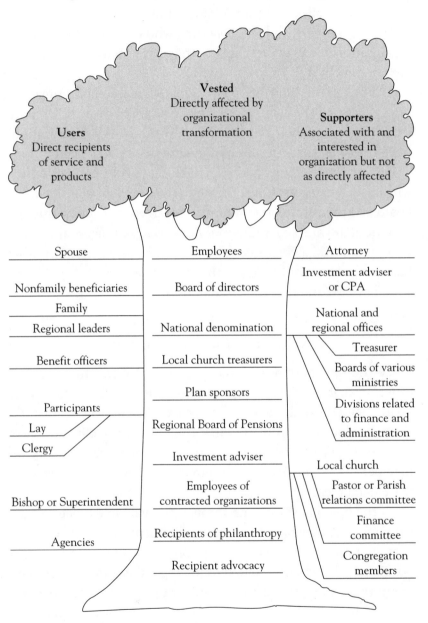

**Vested**
Directly affected by
organizational
transformation

**Users**
Direct recipients
of service and
products

**Supporters**
Associated with and
interested in
organization but not
as directly affected

| Users | Vested | Supporters |
|---|---|---|
| Spouse | Employees | Attorney |
| Nonfamily beneficiaries | Board of directors | Investment adviser or CPA |
| Family | | National and regional offices |
| Regional leaders | National denomination | |
| Benefit officers | Local church treasurers | Treasurer |
| | | Boards of various ministries |
| | Plan sponsors | |
| Participants | | Divisions related to finance and administration |
| Lay | Regional Board of Pensions | |
| Clergy | Investment adviser | |
| | | Local church |
| Bishop or Superintendent | Employees of contracted organizations | Pastor or Parish relations committee |
| | Recipients of philanthropy | Finance committee |
| Agencies | | Congregation members |
| | Recipient advocacy | |

who directly receive the benefits of the organization, (2) *vested entities*, who are affected by any changes in benefits but are not necessarily direct users, and (3) *supporters*, who are associated with the organization and may even help in the service delivery process but are not directly affected by change.

Although this illustration represents a large, complex organization, even smaller organizations may be surprised to see how extensive and diverse their relationship network is. All organizations have the same three groups of constituents. Boards need to look closely at these groups and start making lists of entities falling within each category. Once these relationships are identified, the board can then strategize on how to reach each segment through current board and organizational networks. This figure illustrates how widespread a constituency base may be and emphasizes that board members need to know the market segments of their constituency base and how these relationships tie together.

## Achieving Targeted Position

Once the targeted position has been established, the CEO and other key managers of the organization are important partners with board members as the positioning process begins. Many organizations develop positioning statements identifying leading messages that are important for every organization representative—board member, CEO, manager—to communicate when contact is made with market leaders.

If the board has not gone through the valuable process of developing or reviewing a positioning statement, this may be an important task to complete before communication begins. Most positioning statements are tied to the organization's mission statement; they reflect the organization's unique services and benefits and highlight successful results or data about satisfied customers.

Part of the communication plan should focus on listening to targeted market leaders concerning their current or potential involvement with the organization. If there has been no involvement, then discussions with the market leader (with a heavy emphasis on listening) should focus on

- The organization's mission
- The leader's perception of the market environment
- The needs and wants of the market (and the leader's own needs and wants)
- What the organization is currently providing to the market
- Unique opportunities for service, resources, and partnerships
- Ways each party can exchange value

In this age of relationships, fully engaged board members can no longer rely on the CEO and organization staff to do their listening for them. It is the work of the board to get to know and understand the organization's key users and supporters in order to build strong relationships.

According to an article in the *Harvard Business Review* (Taylor, Chait, and Holland, 1996), "Boards and CEOs have to know what matters to the constituents they serve. The new work requires two-way communication. As a college president remarked, 'Part of the reason for such communication is to make the board vulnerable to constituents, to make it accessible and accountable rather than insulated from the ordinary life of the institution'" (p. 38).

Board members always need to remember that understanding the other individual or organization, instead of rushing to present their own needs, becomes the real core of a long-term, solid relationship. Then, based on understanding the other entity, the next step is to identify their organization's interests in a way that presents potential for support or partnership.

Effective, well-targeted communication is not just a one-time event but a process that includes a variety of strategies and tools, including the relationship with board members, key managers, or other employees of the organization. Consequently, in order to build a strong relationship, each step in the communication process should take place with an awareness of the steps preceding and following the current one. Many board members have experienced initially positive approaches from organizations that seem interested in a possible relationship; however, no subsequent follow-through or contact takes place. This is the way to lose valuable supporters.

In order to build a meaningful relationship, direct contact with the market leader is central to an effective communication plan. The setting for this meeting should be comfortable, convenient, and private—perhaps the leader's home or office—and should be a place where uninterrupted communication can take place. A busy restaurant at lunch time may not be the best choice.

## Targeting Key Relationships in Today's Environment

Most organizations want to identify the leaders of the people they serve and build strong relationships with them. In a social service organization, this may mean parents; it may mean neighborhood and community leaders; or it may mean adults who have benefited from the organization at one point in their lives. For hospitals, it certainly means grateful patients, businesses, and community health interests. Educational institutions will look to former, current, and potential students and to organizations that hire graduates and faculty. Arts groups will look to subscribers or members, as well as artists themselves. Each organization must identify its priority users and the leadership within those groups.

Most nonprofit organizations are supported by both service revenues and gifts or grants from sources with an interest in the mission of the organization. These sources could include individuals, associations, foundations, government, churches, and business or industry. Each source has a leadership group with which organizations must connect to build strong relationships.

Many organizations are finding that an important part of the relationship-building process is collaboration with other groups that can help them deliver value-added services to their constituents.

These groups could include vendors, current competitors, and other knowledge sources. As part of operations planning, organizations should look at these relationships as important positioning tools.

## Collaborating to Increase Value

Jordan Lewis, in his book *Partnerships for Profit: Structuring and Managing Strategic Alliances* (1990), calls collaboration "a relationship between firms in which they cooperate to produce more value than a market transaction" (p. 1).

As this quote suggests, collaboration can generate increased value for the organizations involved. Collaboration involves a commitment to mutual relationships with shared goals and responsibilities. The result is usually shared rewards. In this age of rapid change and diversification, the needs and concerns of one constituency often conflict with the needs and concerns of other constituent groups; however, through well-managed collaboration, both groups may be more successful in achieving their goals than they might have been if they worked in isolation.

Most customer-focused organizations know that maintaining and strengthening relationships with current constituents is far more effective than continually finding new customers and supporters for the organization. This is particularly true for nonprofit organizations in which there are often strongly divergent needs and cultures among program users, supporters, and potential collaborators. (For more information on collaboration, refer to Chapter Six.)

According to Jean Lipman-Blumen in her book on leadership, *The Connective Edge* (1996), readers must work to bring these groups together through strategic communication and relationship building. She says, "If they are to avoid being torn apart by the contradictory needs of various constituencies, leaders will have to bridge enormous cultural divides. They will have to create a sense of community in which a mosaic of organizational members can feel included and impelled to make their special contributions to the total enterprise" (p. 258). This can only be accomplished if there is a strong commitment on the board level to building relationships through listening, communicating, and connecting, both personally and as a leadership group.

## Using Tools for Effective Relationships

Creating relationships is sometimes the most significant challenge a nonprofit board of directors faces. There are formal structures for creating relationships, but many times they're created in informal settings and gatherings. Putting the two together becomes very important. If the board knows the market, many times it can map or begin to identify how to target relationships gathered both formally and informally. Although management may play a key role in identifying relationships, the board needs to be instrumental in accessing those relationships.

An integrated management information system (MIS) can also be used effectively to support an organization's relationship-building efforts. An MIS is simply a tool to give people throughout an organization easy access to the information they need to be high-touch communicators. It provides information with which to begin, enhance, and maintain interpersonal communication, but it is crucial to realize that it cannot replace one-on-one personal contact. An MIS is an important adjunct—not a replacement—to effective, personal communication.

If boards notice any of the following problems within their organizations, it is probably time to implement an MIS or update the current system in order to stay competitive in today's market:

- For no apparent reason, the organization is losing relationships it once had.

- The organization lacks continuity in relationships. It may have good relationships with certain key people but in the process of staff turnover has lost touch with others. Maintaining relationships cannot be too dependent on single individuals.

- Customers work to access the organization, but they don't easily get to the right people or the right services.

- The organization has many relationships, but they aren't producing anything. Board members may be spending lots of time, and the organization may be spending money, with nothing coming back in return.

- The organization communicates well vertically but has significant problems related to horizontal communication among programs, departments, and offices.

- The organization has existing software and hardware that aren't integrated, creating "silos" in programs, departments, or individual sales.

Boards may need to lead management to start the process of learning about customers. When deciding what information is important, start with the basics—name, address, and occupation, as well as phone, fax, and e-mail numbers. Then get family information, such as a spouse's name and occupation and children's names and ages. Note the person's involvement with the organization, including giving and volunteering, as well as particular areas of interest and services used; note other organizations in which he or she is involved. Current and past relationships to the organization are also important.

Various audiences or constituencies need to be identified in a broad sense—for example, donors, service users, alumni, community leaders, and so on. The following questions may be asked:

Who are the organization's audiences now, and who should they be in the future? Then identify individuals within each of these groups.

What processes are currently in place to manage relationships? What's working and what isn't?

What tools are needed to support relationships? Is it more people, more information, new processes, or new technology?

Assessing what an organization has and doesn't have to maintain and build strong relationships is a very important step. Once this level of study has occurred, senior management must be committed to organizing an MIS team to oversee the analysis, development, and implementation of a new system and must be willing to expend capital, time, and human resources to develop state-of-the-art, customer-friendly systems. In the engagement model, it is extremely important for the CEO to inform the board about the progress of developing and using these tools.

## Understanding Constituent Behavior

It is also helpful to understand the varying motivations behind constituent behaviors. Several watershed studies have been published in recent years that shed light on the habits and characteristics of major donors and wealthy individuals. In *The Millionaire Next Door* (Stanley and Danko, 1996), the authors show how the "average" millionaire leads a modest, lower-middle-class lifestyle, contrary to what we might expect from an affluent individual, and that many of those who are living an affluent lifestyle have accumulated little net worth.

*The Seven Faces of Philanthropy* (Prince and File, 1994) illustrates how major donors can be grouped into seven basic personality types. Understanding what motivates each type of donor to give can greatly enhance an organization's relationship-building and resource-development efforts. Building relationships takes time, and the foundation of building relationships is sincere interest in the other party's needs and concerns.

Organizations must continually focus on and refine the service they are providing, but equal emphasis must be directed to creating and maintaining relationships. Most nonprofit organizations exist to serve people. Therefore, people must remain the focus of each and every organization, whether in health care, education, culture, religion, or social services.

People have so many choices today—probably more than ever before—such as where to go to college, which medical center to choose, how to spend their leisure time, or which church to join. In many cases, the service providers who give the customer the most personal treatment will win. Nonprofits can't afford to overlook this fact because it's simply too easy for people to go elsewhere, whether they are service users, donors, or both. In order to achieve and maintain an organization's targeted position in its marketplace, the board must be continually working on maintaining and building relationships, backed up with good information. The organization's mission depends on it.

## Questions for Reflection

How long has it been since your board surveyed constituents and determined your organization's position within the marketplace?

What is your market, and what changes need to be made in your position within that market?

How much emphasis does your board place on developing relationships? Do some board members lack an understanding of their responsibility in bringing new relationships to the organization?

What different relationships should your board be cultivating to enhance your marketplace position?

How will you establish these relationships within your market?

Has your board developed a case statement that reflects the main focus of your positioning efforts?

Do you have an MIS for managing your database of contacts and relationships? If so, is it up-to-date and organized to be helpful to your marketing efforts? If you do not have an MIS, should you consider establishing one?

*Chapter Six*

# Financial Resource Solutions

A foolish consistency is the hobgoblin of little minds.

*Ralph Waldo Emerson*

In this chapter, board members will learn about the importance of integrating a range of resource-generating strategies in today's dynamic nonprofit environment.

As a new board member of a social service organization located in the Pacific Northwest, Bill has dived right into major challenges related to the organization's future. He has been active on an enterprise team that secured philanthropic contributions to research a possible new organizational service—a service with great potential for not only meeting the organization's mission but also generating significant margins. Bill is also excited about the potential for collaborating with another nonprofit in providing this service. Bill says he finds himself enthusiastically engaged in his board activities and is spending much more time than he had originally anticipated on his board involvements. His experience on this board is proving to be very rewarding, and his contributions have made a significant difference in the revenues generated for the agency's charitable activities.

Sally is a long-term and much-valued board member of a high-quality midwestern college. At one point, she started privately expressing her boredom with her board involvement and was considering resigning and joining a more fulfilling organization. However, the board recruited a new president who had been leading the board to launch a number of enterprise initiatives, including a graduate school. Philanthropists are underwriting top professors, and the graduate school is being marketed to local and regional businesses where contracts are emerging to prepare employees for the challenges facing their rapidly changing businesses. Sally is closely involved in the board's planning and philanthropic efforts, which are needed to launch these new enterprises. As a result of Sally's newfound involvement and the board's progressive direction, she is a much more enthusiastic board member and has decided to remain on the board.

In order for an organization to realize its mission, accomplish its goals, and effectively serve its constituencies, it must have sufficient resources. As obvious as this is, some nonprofit boards do not focus as intently as they should on the development of resources. Traditionally, boards have set policies related to resources but were not involved much beyond that and were rarely involved in generating new concepts for resource development; however, in the engagement model of board governance, the board is closely involved in policy and strategic thinking about resources and actively partners with the CEO and senior management to implement revenue generating initiatives.

The reality of course is that resources drive an organization, but which organizations end up with which resources has become a major issue in the increasingly competitive nonprofit arena. In the last decade—primarily because of shifts in the environment and competition among nonprofits—the issue of resource allocation among nonprofits has resulted in groups of "haves" and "have-nots." Today both groups face serious resource issues.

For example, the "haves" include high-quality colleges and universities that, in many cases, have built huge endowments. Until recently, public universities have also been "haves," but that's changing now as traditional sources of support, such as government funding, are shifting and diminishing. If organizations are not careful as these shifts occur, they may find themselves losing their reserves and their margins. In any case, once-thriving nonprofits across the country are asking the question, What will we do about increased costs in light of decreasing revenue? Many times they don't have the answer to this crucial question.

For instance, health care organizations have traditionally been profitable, with very little dependence on philanthropy. Yet currently, as many of them anticipate the end of their profitable business cycles because of a decrease in traditional funding sources and a variety of other industry changes, they realize that an integration of new services, with an increased emphasis on philanthropy and other resource solutions, will be essential to their continued operation.

Those that didn't "have" in the first place are in even deeper trouble. Social services, small to midsize hospitals, long-term care facilities, arts groups, and colleges that never had significant endowments—many of these organizations are facing major challenges to their survival in the future, to say nothing about providing quality care to their constituents. Serious questions have emerged: How are we going to increase and not deplete our reserves? How are we going to cover the services we need to provide to our target markets?

According to an INDEPENDENT SECTOR (Abramson and Salamon, 1997) analysis of the 1998 Congressional Budget Resolution, federal spending in areas of concern to nonprofits will decline 9 percent from 1995 through 2002, representing a cumulative six-year total of nearly $100 billion. In addition, during these six years nonprofits will lose a cumulative total of $50.2 billion of direct federal revenues under the congressional budget package.

And according to the 1996–1997 Nonprofit Almanac (Hodgkinson and Weitzman, 1996), cuts in federal funding will affect all nonprofit organizations, particularly in the areas of community and regional development, international affairs, and social services. The locus of administration for many current programs will continue shifting to state and local governments, resulting in increased competition between nonprofit and for-profit organizations at the state level in contracting for a variety of services in the areas of health care, job training, family services, and residential care.

Nonprofits are confronting these key issues in the context of their dramatically changing environments. Some of these changes are growing out of local trends; others are imposed on communities from national forces. A combination of technology, population trends, economic factors, and political shifts has provided fuel for the pace of change we are experiencing nationwide. Organizations that cannot respond—and respond quickly—to this shift in resources may not survive.

At the same time that resources for funds are shifting, revenue needs are intensifying. Nonprofits must maintain the relevance and currency of their services. In many nonprofit arenas, competition is becoming fierce, and consumers, users, and donors are more willing to shift their alliances if their expectations have not been met. A hospital will quickly lose its edge if it cannot keep pace with technology and innovations. A university that doesn't offer students what they need to succeed in the future will lose support.

Although their customers, students, patients, and donors are demanding more service and more quality, organizations are finding that these same constituents aren't willing to pay increased prices, despite the fact that the organizations' costs are escalating at a frightening rate. New resources have to be found, but every other nonprofit is out looking for many of the same resources. The question is, Who gets what—and how?

As an underlying principle, nonprofits need to first focus on providing good service and then on building a successful resource plan to support the services being provided. Boards need to be directly involved in developing these resource plans. Although many nonprofit boards would say that profit is not their primary goal, at the same time they want to improve their quality of service and grow in their marketplace. Good service and sufficient capital reserves go hand in hand. Most of the time, service can only be improved or expanded with increased resources or reallocation of financial resources. Consequently, as they focus on providing new and enhanced services, boards of nonprofit organizations must also look to new resource solutions. Philanthropy, although still important for supplementing an organization's revenue, is no longer enough in most changing organizations.

## Identifying Resource Solutions

Just as in for-profit businesses, nonprofit organizations need to clearly define current and potential sources of revenue, particularly as they head into a major transformation of programs and services. This is a primary responsibility of a fully engaged board during times of major change. And almost every organization going through such substantive change will need to alter and usually expand the mix of their resource solutions. Organizations don't progress successfully through significant change unless resources are available to take them through the process and provide capitalization for the future. It is essential that an organization's board members, teaming with the CEO and other managers, ensure that sufficient resources are available. The engagement model for board governance calls for a board that has thoroughly investigated and considered five core resource solutions of our time: (1) enterprising, (2) business process redesign, (3) collaboration, (4) philanthropy, and (5) stewardship of resources. These important solutions are described in this chapter.

### Enterprising

*Enterprising* is defined as new or expanded services that produce greater margins, capital to reserves, and could be organized within the existing organization through a new nonprofit or as a for-profit subsidiary. Services provided by the enterprise itself are basic sources of revenue that can be expanded through increased services and increased fees, but organizations also need to look at new or refined entrepreneurial services that enhance their current revenue streams and operating margins, generating reserves for future use. The illustration in Figure 6.1 provides a good visualization of the issues involved

## Figure 6.1.  Building an Enterprise Model

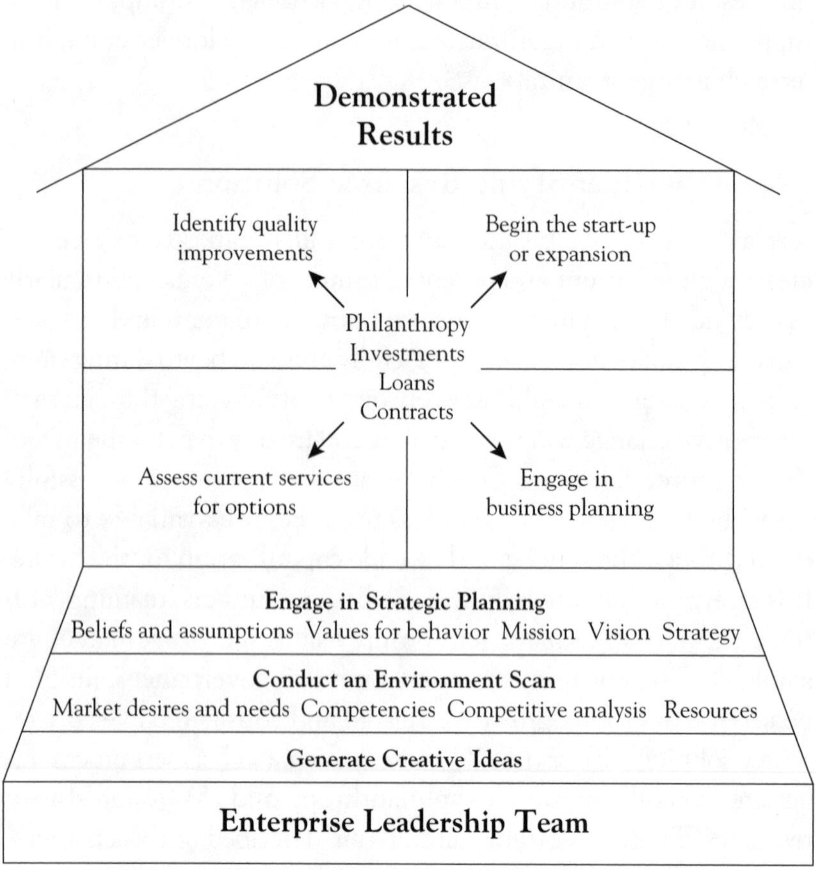

Demonstrated
Results

Identify quality
improvements

Begin the start-up
or expansion

Philanthropy
Investments
Loans
Contracts

Assess current services
for options

Engage in
business planning

**Engage in Strategic Planning**
Beliefs and assumptions  Values for behavior  Mission  Vision  Strategy

**Conduct an Environment Scan**
Market desires and needs  Competencies  Competitive analysis  Resources

**Generate Creative Ideas**

**Enterprise Leadership Team**

in launching a new enterprise, illustrating that an enterprise can fulfill mission and provide resources for an organization to underwrite services that do not pay for themselves.

As Figure 6.1 illustrates, the foundation of an enterprising initiative is an enterprise leadership team, which includes representatives from the board, senior management, and leaders outside the organization, possibly including philanthropists, investors, and constituents. This team engages in three activities:

1. *Generate creative ideas:* Develop concepts for prospective enterprising ventures, which should also include an evaluation of the organization's capacity to provide the new service or product.

2. *Conduct an environment scan:* Review the environment as it may affect the new venture being contemplated, including looking at constituent needs and desires, competencies to pursue this venture within the organization, a competitive analysis of the environment, and a review of the resources needed to support this venture.

3. *Engage in strategic planning:* Review the organization's underlying principles and how they work with the prospective venture, including beliefs and assumptions, values, mission, and vision. This may result in a reevaluation and perhaps refocusing of these principles.

If this thorough review supports embarking on the new enterprising initiative, then the organization will go through the four steps indicated in the model: (1) assessing current services and how they affect the new option, (2) engaging in the necessary business planning for the venture, (3) identifying desired quality improvements, and (4) beginning the actual start-up or expansion. These steps are all supported through various financial resources, including philanthropy, investments, loans, and contracts with outside entities. Ultimately, results will be generated and evaluated.

Goodwill Industries across the country are excellent examples of successful enterprising ventures in a nonprofit setting. Goodwill Industries comprises the world's largest network of privately owned vocational rehabilitation programs and is the world's largest private employer of people with special needs. In particular, Goodwills in Portland, Oregon, and Milwaukee, Wisconsin, are prime examples of enterprise organizations. Although they are nonprofits, they sustain themselves through business operations with major revenue streams. These business operations produce significant profits while supporting their mission and providing capital for future growth and stability.

Michael Miller, president of the Goodwill Industries of Columbia-Willamette, the fastest growing Goodwill in the United States, says, "In an environment in which traditional sources of financial support are threatened, enterprise presents an opportunity to restore, stabilize, and increase funding. Staffing is a key to success. Surround yourself with quality people who can balance mission and business" (*Working Smart*, 1995, p. 2).

John Miller, president of the Goodwill Industries of Southeastern Wisconsin and Metropolitan Chicago, the largest Goodwill in the world, emphasizes that nonprofits wanting to become enterprise organizations should embrace a commitment to planning, the willingness to do things differently to obtain different results, strategic thinking, and a very clear sense of mission and vision. He says, "The more the board, staff, and leadership plan broadly, the more success the organization will have. Every CEO should have a clear understanding of the planning process and revisit that process continually" (*Working Smart*, 1995, p. 2).

In order to launch a new enterprise, the organization should first establish a leadership team. In addition to board members, this team might consist of philanthropists, investors, constituents, and experts within the organization. Board members who are entrepreneurs or business leaders can be especially helpful in launching a new enterprise. The team should look closely at its potential resources, including philanthropy, loans, current contracts, and service revenues and should start assembling the resources needed to begin an enterprise initiative.

Next, an environmental scan should look at the current marketplace, particularly at constituent needs and desires, to ensure that the new enterprise will respond to those needs and to the mission of the organization. Environmental research should also include an analysis of competitors who may already be providing the intended product or service. With this knowledge, the team will be able to start positioning the new enterprise in the marketplace. (Environmental assessments are covered in more detail in Chapter Five.)

Then the team begins to look creatively at its prospective enterprise areas and at its capacity as an organization to provide the new service or product. What kind of internal resources, human and financial, are available to develop the new enterprise? What external resources can help support the new enterprise? Meanwhile, plans for the new venture should be carefully integrated with the organization's current strategic plan, its beliefs, its assumptions, its values, and its mission—all of which can be used as a platform to launch the new enterprise plan.

Once the potential service or product is chosen, more research is needed to test the new venture in the marketplace. Based on the successful outcome of that test, a business plan and financial model are developed for a start-up and expansion. A capitalization plan is then tied to implementation, which can proceed. At the same time, the organization should review its current services and look for any possible quality improvements to provide current customers with higher-quality and better services. It's important for current services to remain at a high level when the organization launches a new enterprise.

The circular chart shown in Figure 6.2 illustrates how capitalization fits into the creation of a new enterprise and emphasizes that capital formation must be integrated into organizational initiatives. The timing should ensure that resources are available as needed for implementation of plans.

This model shows that after an enterprise model has been established (see Figure 6.1), the board needs to approve the plans and related policies. The leadership team has already gone through the key steps of establishing a vision, conducting customer research, and engaging in strategic thinking, which is checked against the organization's mission, goals, and strategy. Then the organization needs to go through the strategic programming and preparation process that will lead to financial modeling and eventually a demonstration, implementation, and evaluation of the new project. Board members need to be involved on the leadership team that oversees this sequence of steps and certainly in the evaluation of the project.

### Figure 6.2. How Capital Formation Fits in Enterprise Creation

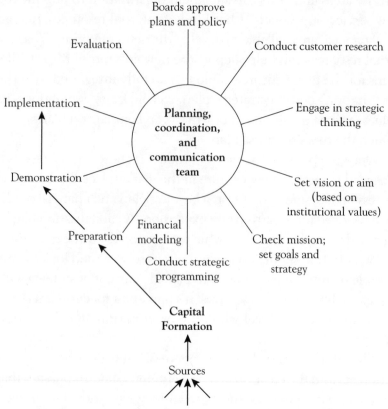

Nonprofits across the country are realizing how important enterprising can be to their resource mix. According to the IRS (2000),

> Taxable profits from unrelated business activities, reported for the Tax Year 1996 by organizations that were otherwise exempt from Federal income taxation, rose 31 percent between 1995 and 1996 and totaled $1.2 billion. The total unrelated business income tax (UBIT) imposed on these profits was $372.6 million, a 35-percent increase over 1995. These increases followed even larger percentage

increases from 1994 to 1995, resulting in an 82-percent increase in total taxable profits and a 94-percent increase in aggregate unrelated business income tax liability for the 2-year period from 1994 to 1996.

The Roberts Foundation in San Francisco, a strong supporter of nonprofit enterprise activity, released a document in late 1996 titled, "New Social Entrepreneurs: The Success, Challenge, and Lessons of Non-Profit Enterprise Creation" (Emerson, 1996). They define a social entrepreneur as "a non-profit manager with a background in social work, community development, or business, who pursues a vision of economic empowerment through the creation of social purpose businesses intended to provide expanded opportunity for those on the margins of our nation's economic mainstream."

A familiar and impressive example of enterprising is a venture undertaken by the well-known Hazelden Foundation, a provider of addiction treatment in Center City, Minnesota. The foundation established a publishing arm that generated significant revenues, allowing Hazelden to maintain low tuition for its high-quality education, prevention, and rehabilitation programs in chemical dependency, even though the organization was experiencing major government funding cutbacks. Meanwhile, similar treatment programs were being dissolved because of decreasing revenues. This amazingly successful enterprising effort had other important benefits for the organization. Hazelden's publishing program produced multiple publications and books in numerous languages that were sold all over the world and created a brand image that promoted and positioned the organization in its marketplace.

Another example is the board of directors of a small, central-city, cultural museum, just five years old, that wanted to develop an internal structure to carry the organization through as a business first and then build credibility within the donor and business community. To plan for this restructuring and growth, the newly hired executive director, with some outside guidance, led the board through a self-assessment process and reorganization that included designing a new mission, purpose, and bylaws. Following a board retreat, new thinking emerged and more business-oriented board members were recruited and elected. Many passionate conversations and productive meetings resulted in creative ideas for growth and development.

The executive director and board of directors realized it was imperative to become self-sustaining and to earn more revenue toward reinvestment for future growth. The money raised by the board of directors financed capital improvements and more than doubled the museum's original size and staff. These improvements provided an opportunity to explore enterprising solutions. One such opportunity occurred because the growth of the museum had created the capacity to bring in a popular traveling exhibit, increasing the museum's visibility and drawing a larger audience of visitors.

Another well-prepared enterprising solution was the development of a museum gift shop, where visitors can browse and purchase unique gifts and souvenirs related to the museum's cultural focus. Gifts can also be purchased on-line through a new e-commerce opportunity available on their Web site.

Furthermore, as the museum's enterprising mission grows, it continues to build on its early revenue-building strategies by leasing the building for wedding receptions, parties, business events, and other occasions. The director of the museum has commented that with a business mind-set, one can see opportunities that never would have been thought of before. Through enterprising services, this cultural organization has become self-sustainable and well positioned for further growth.

As this example emphasizes, enterprising is first and foremost an attitude. It's a way of looking at what an organization has that is valuable and then developing a business around that service or product in a way that serves the organization and the marketplace. The board of directors of a nonprofit organization has a key role in establishing this enterprising attitude and then providing leadership for the research and planning that leads to implementation of new revenue-generating ventures.

## Business Process Redesign

Called reengineering in the for-profit sector, process redesign seeks to create efficiencies and reallocate resources to more productive areas within an organization. Sometimes the words *transformation* and *process redesign* are used interchangeably because process redesign usually means dramatic shifts and changes in the way an organization operates. Although process redesign or reengineering is a common approach for businesses in the corporate world that are looking for ways to become more productive, process redesign is still a fairly new concept in the nonprofit arena. However, the time has come for fully engaged nonprofit boards to learn from business and review their procedures and productivity as they embrace change and seek to use their resources more wisely. As pointed out in earlier chapters, nonprofits can benefit greatly by running their organizations in a more businesslike fashion while not compromising their missions. This may not be easy for many nonprofit organizations. Process redesign may result in the abandonment of some programs (a difficult step for most nonprofits), dramatic changes in other programs, and the commencement of new programs.

Michael Hammer, who coined the word *reengineering* in the late 1980s, defined the term as "the radical redesign of business processes for dramatic improvement." He points out in his book, *Reengineering the Corporation* (Hammer and Champy, 1993), "The key word in the definition is 'process': a complete end-to-end set of activities that together create value for a customer" (p. xii). He goes on to observe, "For a world of process-centered organizations everything must be rethought: the kinds of work that people do, the jobs they hold, the skills they need, the ways in which their performance is measured and rewarded, the careers they follow, the roles managers play, the principles of strategy that enterprises follow" (p. xii).

In *Reengineering Health Care* (1994), authors David Zimmerman and John Skalko emphasize that reengineering is not a dramatic breakthrough in management thinking. It is a refinement of process improvement, technology, and methodology that draws from previous thinking. Reengineering reinvents. The factors that motivate a company to embark on reengineering can vary widely, but virtually all center around change.

As these experts point out, redesigning centers on how work is done, not on how an organization is structured. Reengineering uses technology to enable new process designs, not to provide new mechanisms for performing old tasks.

Boards of directors have a major responsibility to work with their CEOs and senior management to determine whether their organization needs to redesign their processes. Not only is it obviously good operating procedure to make sure the organization is operating as efficiently as possible, it is especially important for philanthropists today to know that their recipient organizations are being well managed. Today's baby boomer donors, in particular, rarely give without first studying how well organizations are run.

An article in *Time* emphasizes this point very clearly:

> Silicon Valley CEOs, along with other newly rich Americans, are finally stepping up to the collection plate. And just as they've transformed American business, members of this new generation are changing the way philanthropy is done. Most are very hands on. They do lots of research before giving. They demand accountability and results. . . . Many of today's tech millionaires and billionaires are applying to philanthropy the lessons they have learned as entrepreneurs. They want to make sure their charitable investments benefit their ultimate customers—those in need—and don't get lost in red tape and bureaucracy. [Greenfeld, 2000, p. 49]

Nonprofit boards typically embark on reengineering for one of the following three reasons:

1. *They have no choice.* They are at the edge of the financial abyss and will fall in if they do nothing.

2. *They see trouble coming.* Everything is going fine, but there is a wall up ahead that will prevent future growth.

3. *They want to stay ahead.*

Nonprofit boards that are aware of the need for transformation well in advance of being pushed to the abyss will be most successful in their oversight of redesign efforts. The role of the board is to ask appropriate questions of the CEO about the status of the activity (resource solution) to determine the timing and direction of process redesign in order to achieve quality, process efficiencies, cost savings, and customer satisfaction. It is not in the public interest for an organization to find itself at a point of no choice; rather, process redesign should take place when the organization is strong and has options.

For example, a social service agency board of directors surveyed constituents concerning their perception of the agency. They discovered a major problem in the agency's mail program that was negatively affecting the perception that donors and community leaders had about the organization. The organization had twelve different mailing lists that were not interconnected. People were receiving duplicate mailings (or more) or not receiving mailings at all. Address corrections were called in again and again but still didn't register (a significant problem, as almost 16 percent of the U.S. population moves each year [U.S. Census Bureau, 1999]). Names were misspelled, and key contributors received mailings that should not have been targeted to them and didn't receive others. The resulting image being created was of a poorly run, wasteful organization. As a result, the agency created one database with an effective address change process. This may seem like such a simple step, but it was actually crucial to the effectiveness of its communication process with its constituents and donors. Not only was the agency's position in the community dramatically enhanced but significant cost efficiencies were achieved. (See Exhibit 6.1 for the steps in the redesign process.)

**Exhibit 6.1. Basic Steps in the Redesign Process**

1. The board, CEO, and key managers commit to business redesign, selecting appropriate assistance.
2. The leaders communicate the organization's commitment to redesign and define the benefits.
3. Leadership connects the redesign process to planning and the process of change.
4. Leadership forms an action team to head the redesign effort.
5. The organization identifies its current business processes.
6. The organization's leaders listen to customers and express results, both qualitatively and quantitatively.
7. The action team prioritizes the changes that need to be made.
8. The action team selects and empowers team leaders.
9. The action team develops redesign teams.
10. Leadership creates financial projections.
11. The action team demonstrates changes.
12. Leadership implements changes.
13. Leadership evaluates, refines, and revamps redesign as necessary.

Copyright © Growth Design Corporation, 2002

Once a redesign effort is launched, the redesign teams should ask the following questions:

How can this be done faster?

How can this be done for less?

What if this isn't done at all?

What is this work for?

What is the goal of this strategy or tactic?

What is the market?

Who is the customer?

How can this work better?

*Changes That May Take Place as a Result of Process Redesign:*

- Work units change—from functional departments to process teams.
- Jobs change—from simple tasks to multidimensional work.
- People's roles change—from controlled to empowered.
- Job preparation changes—from training to education.
- Focus of performance measures and compensation shifts— from activity to results.
- Advancement criteria change—from performance to ability.
- Values change—from protective to productive.
- Organizational structures change—from hierarchical to flat.
- Executives change—from scorekeepers to leaders.
- Workload changes—from overworked employees to greater efficiency.
- Potential cost savings (although this may not be a primary goal of reengineering).

Boards should not embark on the redesign process without being aware of the great risks involved. The redesign process can become very convoluted, and the ultimate goal lost in the process. George Starcher (2000), in his Internet article *Socially Responsible Enterprise Restructuring*, points out,

> When done responsibly, reengineering can produce dramatic improvements in customer service, quality, and productivity. However, reengineering often fails to result in these benefits. As shown in a survey of 99 completed reengineering initiatives undertaken in 1994, two-thirds were judged to produce mediocre, marginal or failed results. There are a number of reasons for these poor results. Perhaps most important are the lack of attention to the human dimension, poor communications, and the fear, stress, and anxiety created. Other reasons include unrealistic expectations, inadequate

resources (quality and quantity of staff and consultants involved), short-term results orientation, and lack of sponsorship.

As they lead their organizations through the redesign process, boards should keep in mind that the process is being redesigned first for the customer and not for the organization. For example, a large suburban church recently expanded and redesigned its parking lot because surveys had shown that attendance had been affected by a lack of easily accessible parking. However, a new visitor to the church could not find a parking place, even though there were many empty parking places close to the front door. These parking places were marked "reserved" for various levels of pastors and associate pastors, the choir directors, and quite a few program directors. Yet no places were set aside for visitors. The first impression the visitor had was that the church was inhospitable.

In an equally unwelcoming situation, a large hospital has very limited parking—so limited that many times patients cannot find a place to park. When they do find a place, there is a significant charge. Meanwhile, a competing hospital in the same community has implemented valet parking at no charge. Guess which hospital imparts the most positive and friendly image to the patient? If this parking lot situation were examined as part of a thorough process redesign, the problem would undoubtedly be identified and could be solved, perhaps making a substantial difference in the hospital's community position and its bottom line.

In redesigning resource solutions, nonprofit boards need to be wary of making assumptions about funding sources that may change. Organization leaders need to stay on top of funding trends. For instance, government funding for all nonprofits has shifted or dramatically decreased over the past decade, and those shifts and decreases will continue. Nonprofits that have been heavily dependent on government funding need to look at a different mix of resource solutions; however, it is important to realize that the trend has been for funding to move from the national level to state and local levels. This may open up more doors for organizations that can convince their local funders to support them, emphasizing even more the importance of positive positioning and public relations within the local community.

### Collaboration

Collaboration occurs when an organization forms alliances and partnerships in which resources are pooled to add value to a certain customer base in providing services and products. The concept of collaboration is growing in the nonprofit sector as a means for organizations to realize resource goals they may not be able to accomplish alone, with the ultimate goal of creating added value for the customer. For-profit organizations have recognized the importance of collaboration for some time, and board members with experience in business collaboration can be especially valuable to nonprofits embarking on collaborative efforts. The stage needs to be set for collaborative efforts by an organization's board of directors.

The question is, Collaborate with whom? The key to any effective collaboration is that both partners have congruent missions and values, as well as similar cultures and interests. There are several key points to contemplate when selecting collaborative partners:

- All organizations involved in collaborative efforts must be willing to yield benefits to partners.
- Risk must be shared by all partners.
- Mutual needs should be addressed.
- The organizations involved should have common objectives in pursuing the collaboration.

In order to choose the right collaborative partners, an organization must first know itself well. So it might be a good idea to submit to a complete organizational assessment (as described in Chapter Seven). If an organization doesn't understand itself, then it will obviously have trouble communicating who and what it is to a prospective partner. The organizations considering collaboration should also sense a chemistry or synergy with each other. Do they share the same culture, the same financial and strategic styles? Are the organizations compatible historically, philosophically, and strategically?

When the right partners collaborate, all parties should reap considerable benefits, including the sharing of both risks and resources. Collaborative partners also learn from each other and find that their individual organizations are strengthened by the partnership. As a new entity, they may find that they are better able to stay ahead of the curve when it comes to meeting client needs and that they have a distinct competitive advantage.

Paul W. Mattessich and Barbara R. Monsey, in *Collaboration: What Makes It Work* (1992), point out that a collaboration is "a mutually beneficial and well-defined relationship entered into by two or more organizations to achieve common goals. The relationship includes: a commitment to mutual relationships and goals; a jointly developed structure and shared responsibility; mutual authority and accountability for success; and sharing of resources and rewards" (p. 7).

However, there can be downsides to collaborative efforts if they are not properly conceived. There can be significant front-end costs and human resource demands. Consequently, collaborative organizations need to make sure their plans have adequately accounted for these factors. Although good collaborations should increase operating efficiencies, sometimes just the opposite happens if organizations have not eliminated duplications of efforts.

Organizations are sometimes concerned about loss of their intellectual property. Clear guidelines need to be established about ownership of shared materials. There is sometimes a risk of one organization dominating the other and eventually taking it over; however, this possibility can be avoided if it is anticipated and barriers to this possibility are established in the initial legal structure of the collaboration. Finally, although a nonprofit board may have the highest hopes for the success of its collaborative efforts, there is always the possibility that it will not meet expectations in the marketplace. Boards need to be realistic when setting their goals.

Many of these potential problems can be avoided if boards are aware of some of the key mistakes others have made when launching collaborative efforts. The most common mistake is choosing an incompatible partner, as discussed earlier. Beyond those points, there should be a sense of camaraderie and shared excitement for the venture among prospective partners that is difficult to quantify. Boards may also encounter problems unless the CEO is a complete partner, completely and enthusiastically committed to the collaboration. When this situation exists, boards need to either change their CEO's thinking, find a new CEO, or consider not entering into the collaboration in the first place.

Undercapitalization of the initiative is also a common problem, which means financial models need to be very clearly developed so that resources for meeting the initiative's goals are clearly in place. Boards need to ask the CEO for well-defined financial and program expectations that are conservative and within the realm of what is realistically possible. Finally, collaborations should always plan an exit strategy. Many organizations have found themselves floundering unnecessarily because they had no idea how to cease their operation and relationships.

An excellent example of a successful collaborative effort started with a ten-thousand-member church located on two hundred acres in the southwestern United States. In an effort to broaden their impact in their marketplace and to add revenue streams to their bottom line, the board of the church decided to form a nonprofit development company, which brought in partners to offer services that would be compatible with the church's values and mission. As a result of the board's foresight, a wide range of new ventures have materialized or are under way.

A school, beginning in preschool and continuing through high school, was established on the church's property. A long-term care organization developed an assisted living and nursing home facility in conjunction with the church. A college consortia is in the process of developing a college campus on the church's property. A memorial chapel and cremation cemetery is another addition. A large church worship center has been added. A collaborative partner is building a hotel resort, which will include a leadership institute. Another corporation has been invited to provide a restaurant and food court on the campus. All these endeavors come under the umbrella of the development organization established by the board, supporting its goals and mission while helping to financially support its programs. Increased revenues have allowed the church to substantially support its charitable endeavors, and all the new programs and services have attracted many more people to the church and its activities, reinforcing the church's mission in the community.

## Philanthropy

Gifts and grants for capital, annual, and endowment support are used to underwrite or subsidize operations or enhancements of programs, facilities, and technology; however, significant changes in donor profiles are taking place in the philanthropic arena. Donors are demanding to know more about where their dollars are going and the results that have occurred. Giving without seeing is diminishing. These new donors want high-touch involvement with direct benefits. This trend is based in part on an escalating mistrust people have about nonprofits and the way their funds are used. Numerous organizations are competing for the same donor dollars, and donors are becoming more selective about their recipients.

It is important for board members in today's nonprofits to realize that they set the stage for philanthropy by being donors themselves. Because board members are representatives of the community in their role on an organization's board, they become symbols of attitudes around public trust. Therefore, in principle, if board members approve the use of philanthropy as a resource solution, they should contribute (to their full capacity) to the organization as a symbol of their commitment. If board members approve philanthropy as a solution and don't themselves give, they send the community a confusing signal that makes fundraising difficult. Board members who don't give are suggesting to the community that something is amiss that prevents them from giving. Most organizations publish annual reports that tell who is giving and (by omission) who is not. It's not unusual for potential donors to look at these reports to see how a board is giving before making a decision to support an organization.

The full support of the board is even more important as we consider some of these major trends that will affect nonprofit organizations in the future:

- *The growth, in both asset size and resulting influence, of community and other foundations.* Particularly important are the sale of nonprofit health care institutions to for-profit ventures.
- *The shift in corporate funding from philanthropic giving to marketing partnerships.* A report published by the Council on Foundations proposes that corporations are more likely to give to programs that can be shown to directly improve their bottom lines and suggests ways in which nonprofit organizations can quantify the results of corporate giving.
- *The increasing potential of publicly funded agencies competing for private gifts.* These three watershed gifts to traditionally publicly funded organizations in 1996–97 have raised the specter of government competition for private gifts: H. J. Heinz Company gave $450,000 to the National Endowment for the Arts; Ted Turner pledged $1 billion to the United Nations; and George Soros committed $500 million to develop aid programs in Russia.

According to *Giving USA 2000* (AAFRC Trust for Philanthropy, 2000), 43 percent of all charitable support in the United States in 1999 was given to religious organizations. This is down from a high of roughly 55 percent of all giving in the early 1980s. Educational organizations received 14.4 percent of all gifts in 1999, whereas health care organizations received 9.4 percent, human services causes received 9.1 percent, and arts, culture, and humanities organizations received 5.8 percent of charitable gifts.

The board's role in developing philanthropy as a resource solution is more important now than ever before. An example of a board assuming this important role involves a museum and cultural center dedicated to celebrating and preserving the history and culture of a specific country's heritage. This museum's board was engaged in planning for a capital campaign. A study was conducted to test the feasibility of raising over $20 million for the museum.

Early interviews with constituents indicated that the vision and plans for the museum were warmly embraced by an overwhelming majority of those interviewed. Findings indicated a strong supportive attitude toward the museum and its executive director; however, feedback suggested that the board and senior staff were less well known in the community and that the campaign leadership was not expected to come from the current board. Some constituents viewed the board of directors as taking a wait-and-see attitude, lacking visibility and connections to wealth in the community. Another key finding of the study was that nearly all the constituents interviewed said they would be willing to consider their own gift, but no interviewees identified themselves as potential campaign leaders, meaning that there was still more relationship work to do before enlistment could begin with confidence.

With this in mind, the board and executive director realized that, given the older age and financial situation of many potential campaign donors, it was necessary to immediately begin action to cultivate and solicit gifts. The organization realized that it must act promptly or it would lose forever the potential for significant gifts from long-standing friends of the cultural center, for whom their background and involvement had been a cornerstone of their life experience.

The board of directors realized that they would probably not be able to play the role of lead wealth generator, but they could provide solid gift support and enthusiastic communication and endorsement. It was crucial for the board to demonstrate its commitment to the project and its organization's vision through a more active role in cultivation and solicitation activity. The museum's leaders realized they would need to engage prospective donors more deeply and more regularly than ever before. One action step that came out of this realization was to enlist close friends and influencers to each host a small group of friends to identify and develop individuals for eventual solicitation. Figure 6.3 outlines this donor development process.

Board members would also need to demonstrate their own commitment through personal financial contributions.

**Figure 6.3.  Major Donor Development Process**

Relationship Continuum

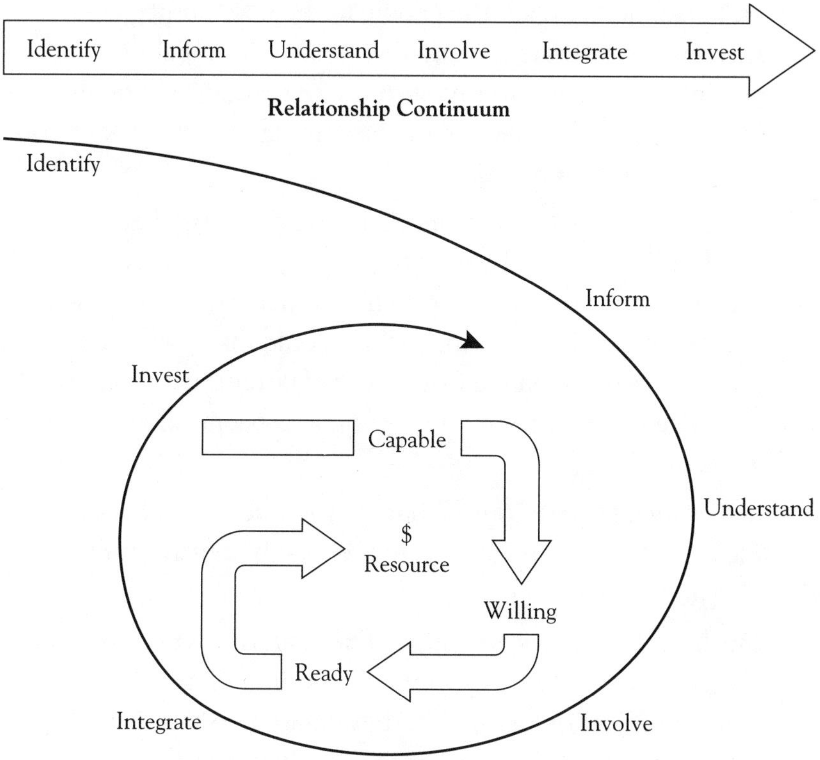

Resource Development Continuum

In this example, the organization built on the current strengths of the board, executive director, and organization as a whole in developing a successful capital campaign. Out of the feasibility study findings, they also had valuable information for future board development issues related to relationship building and resource development for this growing museum and cultural center.

Figure 6.3 illustrates an effective major donor development process—a process that focuses on finding donors who are capable of making contributions, are willing to make contributions, and are ready to make contributions. The process of developing this kind of donor involves the following five steps:

1. *Identify appropriate potential donors.* This is a key board activity, performed in partnership with the CEO and an advancement professional. Who are the people in the community, constituent base, or target market who have the capability and possible inclination to invest in the organization? These might be members of constituency groups, community or corporate leaders, or past donors.

2. *Inform them about the organization.* These potential donors need to be aware of the mission, programs, and outcomes of the organization before they will consider any level of involvement. This informing process could take place one-on-one with board members, or groups of potential donors could be invited to an informational program specifically targeted at them.

3. *Understand who they are.* What are their beliefs, values, interests, capabilities, and connectedness to the organization's mission and values?

4. *Involve them in the organization.* They can be invited to special programs, receptions, and annual meetings or asked to tour a specific project or facility. Or they could be asked to work for the organization. The deeper the involvement, the stronger the investment.

5. *Integrate them much more closely into the organization.* Once these prospects have had some involvement and are responding positively, they can be integrated further into the organization's activities. Their advice can be solicited in their areas of expertise, or they can be asked to sit on an ad hoc committee. If appropriate, some key leaders can even be asked to sit on the board.

6. *Invest them in the organization so that they feel an ownership or sense of responsibility related to the organization.* The more prospects become involved and feel they have made important contributions, the more invested they will feel in the organization. At this point, they may be willing to invest more of themselves in a variety of ways and can be approached for a donation.

### Stewardship of Resources

A person who demonstrates good stewardship takes the responsibility of being entrusted with another's property, money, and confidential information very seriously. Whether managing an office, cultivating a potential donor, or gathering personal information, this person must value treating these resources with great confidentiality, care, and respect. The same philosophy applies to the stewardship of resources, which is the responsibility of a nonprofit board of directors. Although boards should not be actively managing finances and investments, they should play an oversight role, making sure that they are aware of what is happening and that resources are being handled judiciously for the public trust.

Optimum management of resources produces more resources for an organization and is key to an organization's healthy financial picture. Unfortunately, nonprofit boards have not always paid attention to this crucial responsibility. In fact, many boards are not even aware of what their resources are and how they're being managed. For example, many colleges and other organizations own valuable but unproductive land that sits idle. Fortunately, many of these organizations are starting to look at their land and facilities and consider how they might be used more productively. By becoming better stewards of their resources, boards bolster their organization's financial strength, which translates into better services for customers and a stronger institution.

For instance, some colleges are inviting other organizations or businesses to use their land for both nonprofit and for-profit purposes. Fast-food restaurants, retirement villages, financial services, and travel agencies on college campuses are providing additional services for students while sharing their revenues with the institutions.

Ironically, the oversight of the management of a nonprofit's financial assets is a key board responsibility that is often not handled professionally or with a strong sense of stewardship. Volunteers, who are frequently inexperienced in financial management, are managing large assets of land, money, and endowments. Many times these volunteers are producing much lower returns on their investments than are standard in the industry. It should also be noted that there is a serious potential conflict of interest when a board member manages an organization's assets. More astute boards are bringing in professional financial managers to manage their investments and generate higher returns.

Stewardship of human resources is another area that warrants careful board attention. When employees are underpaid, resulting in high turnover and increased training costs, the organization suffers. When computer systems are out of date, labor costs increase and redundancies occur. Good management of people and systems relates directly to good management of financial resources.

Boards need to request that their CEOs look closely at their people, dollars, land, and facilities and then ask themselves, What do we have that is of value? and Are we using our resources to their fullest potential to benefit our mission and to serve the public trust? A starting point may be for the board to ask the CEO to produce an asset description, including reports on how each asset is being used and recommendations on how each asset could be used to a better advantage for the organization.

## Integrating Resource Solutions

When fully engaged boards of nonprofits look at these five key resource solutions—enterprising, business process redesign, collaboration, philanthropy, and stewardship of resources—as part of an integrated plan, each solution gains strength. Too often in the past, organizations have used these solutions in isolation from each other. When resource solutions are treated as silos that exist vertically, not touching each other, it is impossible to receive the maximum benefit from each solution. For instance, when donors make contributions because of good service, the service arm of an organization should be working closely with philanthropy to identify giving opportunities and ensure that the service being provided meets the expectations of the prospective donor. A good example is St. Luke's Medical Center, a large hospital in the Milwaukee area that has a highly successful giving program highlighted by significant numbers of multimillion-dollar gifts, where there is a close working relationship among the medical enterprise, the physicians, and the philanthropy officers.

Donors today are very sophisticated and are looking for organizations to be efficient and prudent in their use of resources. When they see an organization going through reengineering or process redesign, they are likely to be impressed with efforts to control expenses. An atmosphere is created that is more conducive to giving. It is also essential to look for common interests in choosing partners for sharing resources. By asking a local business what its needs are related to the college or hospital or social service agency, a partnership evolves where new services are developed that meet the needs of the enterprise and its constituency. Customers and donors alike need to know they will be reaping maximum value and benefits from their investment of time and resources.

The first step in developing a successful resource plan is to get the service right. This demands constant research and listening to the wants, needs, and desires of constituents. In a fast-paced, changing environment, this is a constant task. Boards need ongoing updates on what their customers are saying about their needs, perceptions, and levels of service satisfaction. Successful resource solutions are fundamentally based on providing the appropriate service for the target market.

## Implementing Solutions

Organizations need to look carefully at their potential resource solutions, identifying and prioritizing them in relation to their overall organizational direction and plan. For each solution to become a viable resource option, the eight elements illustrated in Figure 6.4 need to be tied to an overall plan and financial model.

Elements for successful resource development are as follows:

- *Leadership Development:* The group leading the solution initiative needs to be identified and organized, both externally and internally. This leadership group will oversee policy, management, and implementation of the solution.
- *Planning and Modeling:* The solutions need to be integrated into the organization's overall strategies and plans.
- *Market Research:* Listening to the customer in relation to the solution is essential. Equally important is the need for an organization to understand how it is perceived in the market. The target market should be profiled and tested. The solution needs to be packaged to appeal to the market.
- *Communication:* The solution needs to be effectively communicated to both internal (employees, volunteers) and external constituents so they understand how the solution will affect them.
- *Human Resources and Information Technology:* The solution needs to be tied to the infrastructure of human resources that will implement the initiative. The organization should plan and establish a system for the use of technology and information management.

Figure 6.4.  Resource Development Wheel

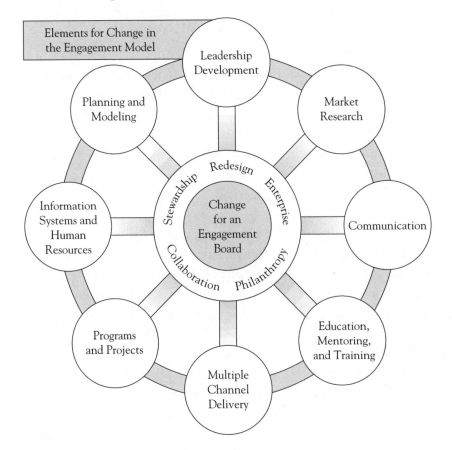

- *Programs and Projects:* The new solution process should be integrated with already existing programs, including philanthropy or fund development, marketing and communication, reengineering, and business development.

- *Education, Mentoring, and Training:* Education, training, and orientation should be carefully planned for everyone involved in the solution planning and implementation, including employees, leaders, and volunteers. The result will be a strengthening of individual abilities and competencies so that those assigned specific responsibilities will be successful in their new or modified roles.

- *Multiple Resource Channel Delivery:* Leaders know the importance of sustaining strong relationships through "multiple channel delivery" with those who want to know about, participate in, and support their missions. Multiple channel delivery techniques include the use of Web and electronic communication, direct response marketing, face-to-face meetings, special events, and grant proposals.

Many organizations look at one or more of these elements but fail to see each element as a critical part of an entire process necessary for the effective development of any resource solution. For instance, an organization may decide to launch a philanthropic initiative, such as a capital campaign, but neglect to plan for the human and capital resources needed to implement the campaign. Or perhaps they've failed to connect the initiative to good communication channels. Any missing link can lead to failure of the initiative. All these elements need to be integrated into a comprehensive plan in order for the solution to be optimally successful. The board has a crucial role in helping the organization determine the appropriate mix of resource solutions to emphasize.

## Questions for Reflection

What are your organization's current primary sources of funding? Does your organization rely on one or two traditional fundraising methods, such as special events or direct mail, for the majority of its revenue?

Do your revenue streams from current services and products have potential for growth, or is a major overhaul needed?

What changes have taken place during the past few years in the resources that support your organization? What changes in funding sources do you foresee in the future?

Do fewer than 100 percent of your board members contribute to the organization in significant ways, monetarily or through bringing other major contributions into the organization?

Are any of the resource solutions suggested in this chapter not being used by your organization? Which ones? Could these solutions be effective for your organization?

Have the words *enterprise* or *collaboration* been mentioned at any of your recent board meetings?

What steps does your board need to take to implement new resource solutions?

Do your board members understand how your organization's funds are being managed? How long has it been since this fund management has been evaluated?

*Chapter Seven*

# Performance Evaluation

One of the tests of leadership is the ability to
recognize a problem before it becomes an
emergency.

*Arnold Glasgow*

In this chapter, board members will learn about the importance of
assessing the performance of the organization's leadership, including its CEO and the board itself. They will also understand what
steps need to be taken in order to achieve a thorough assessment
that can be applied to strategies for future development.

Dorothy is board chair of a statewide food storage and distribution organization. As she prepares to pass the baton to a new chair, she realizes there are some issues related to who that chair should be. She
believes the organization's new business plan calls for a chair of the
future having a different profile than in the past; in fact, she believes
the board should redefine itself in light of the new direction. As a result, Dorothy, with the CEO and a small group of board members,
leads a board assessment process that reviews eleven areas related to
the board's job and function. The goal is to develop a report and a set
of recommendations, including a profile of the kind of chair and
board members needed to lead the organization in the future.
Dorothy is excited about the resulting report and is currently working closely with the new chair, who was selected on the basis of the
new profile, to help him assume his position with a clear understanding of the direction that the board should be taking in the future.

David has been the CEO of a Catholic seminary for several years. When he was recruited, clear guidelines were established by the board related to the direction the organization and its board wanted for the future. David then established his own directions and specific strategies related to the overall mission and vision of the organization. He met with a small board team on a monthly basis and, through a productive and positive interactive process, was able to develop evaluative material that was presented and summarized at board meetings. When his formal, annual evaluation occurred, there were no surprises, and the process went smoothly because a regular evaluative communication process was already established, thus enhancing his growth and development at the seminary.

Organizational change demands a rethinking of leadership and how it functions in relationship to the changes being implemented. Especially in dynamic, changing organizations, boards must know how their leadership is performing at all levels. The engagement model of board leadership identifies evaluation as a key board responsibility. Traditional nonprofit boards have always been involved in CEO evaluation, but that was basically all boards did in the form of evaluation. Today's fully engaged board members understand that they need to regularly assess their own performance and the performance of individual board members, as well as the CEO and the organization itself.

More and more nonprofits and their national associations are partnering to develop assessment tools to use regularly for self-assessment; the goal is to give themselves and their key managers feedback related to leadership performance and how it can be changed and improved. In addition, organizations are increasingly beginning to tie compensation plans to performance indicators.

One key factor in this intensified focus on assessment is that funding sources and major donors are starting to demand proof of effective governance. The process of assessment then becomes closely tied to an organization's fundraising initiatives. Assessment is also closely related to how services are developed and delivered.

As a result, there may be a wide constituency outside an organization, including donors and customers, who need the assurance that some kind of effective evaluation is going on inside an organization. This increasing demand for assessment has resulted in a proliferation of evaluation tools.

The media regularly present stories about for-profit and non-profit organizations whose boards did not carefully monitor performance indicators for their CEOs and other key leaders. Stories also proliferate about boards themselves that were not performing up to their capabilities and about organizations that may close their doors because of waning resources or operational dysfunction. These scenarios are frequently the result of lack of assessment. An organization that does not assess and plan its leadership is, in a sense, like an airplane flying without instruments or a flight plan in cloudy weather. Who knows where the plane is going or where it will land? Likewise, leadership operating without assessment may find itself flying blind and inevitably missing the mark when it comes to meeting goals and objectives.

There are really two evaluations that board members need to concentrate on. One is an evaluation of the CEO and the other is evaluation of the board itself. In addition, many boards are now asking for regular organizational and service outcome assessments.

## Looking at the Board

When most board members are asked about performance evaluation within their organizations, they are quick to point out the importance of evaluating the CEO. Board members do not always recognize the need to evaluate themselves. However, in growing numbers of nonprofit organizations, boards are beginning to realize how crucial that is. After all, a board is the top governing body of an organization—a body with authority over the CEO and responsibility for carrying out the organization's mission. Therefore, it is crucial that the board be held to certain performance standards that have been carefully established.

It is particularly important for a board to be assessed as the organization embarks on an intense process of change. A board needs to be positioned to engage in ongoing policy review, strategic thinking, and continuous planning. The board needs to make sure that all its crucial roles, as well as its structure, are in place so that it is ready to function as a strong and effective leadership group.

## Investigating Available Tools

A variety of effective tools are available for board self-assessment, including assessment tools produced by the Center for Nonprofit Management, the Association of Governing Boards of Colleges and Universities, the American Management Association, and the National Center for Nonprofit Boards. Industry associations may also produce specifically focused assessment tools that can be very helpful. A variety of sources for board, CEO, and organizational assessment are listed in the Resources section in the Appendix.

In addition, some boards that govern unique organizations with specialized needs have decided to create their own assessment tools. This is a particularly challenging and time-consuming endeavor because it involves the development and analysis of the tool and the interpretation and communication of the results.

The process of finding and using an assessment tool may start with the hiring of an outside consultant or an objective third party with human resources experience. Although some organizations have launched successful internal board assessments, boards should be aware of the risks involved. No matter how well-intentioned a completely internal team may be, it is difficult to remain totally objective and unbiased during the evaluation process. As a result, a board runs the risk of creating a divisive atmosphere among board members. Although the intent should not be to implicate any one person, this can happen all too easily without outside objectivity guiding the process.

It is important to emphasize, however, that in a board or CEO evaluation process the board of directors always needs to remain in charge. An outside consultant may work with a small steering team (three to five members) from the board itself and the CEO. This team selects a tool for self-evaluation and oversees its implementation. Some board members may be uncomfortable with the evaluation. Therefore, team members need to speak regularly to their peers on the board about the importance and need for this kind of evaluation once it is organized, and all comments will be anonymous and held in confidence. Team members should also identify the tool they are planning to use, define the anticipated process and timetable, and enlist cooperation among board members to implement the assessment process.

The resulting responses to the assessment tool are typically sent to a third party outside the board and the organization for analysis; many assessment tools are now analyzed by computer. Then capable team members or third parties take the analysis, interpret it, and develop a report with recommendations that goes back to the steering team. Once the team has reviewed and accepted the report, it is finalized and presented to the board, frequently at a retreat. The board uses this report to develop an agenda for the future that focuses on improving its performance. Boards that regularly assess their performance can also compare current performance to earlier assessments and recommendations.

## Covering Key Areas

Whatever instrument is selected for evaluation, organizations should cover certain basic areas during the assessment process. A thorough assessment should look closely at the areas listed next, identifying strengths and problems. The board can then go through a problem-solving process around the issues identified.

- Identifying, recruiting, orienting, and retaining board members
- Establishing efficient board structures and processes
- Developing and maintaining ethical guidelines for board members

- Communicating with other board members, CEO, staff, and constituents
- Defining and carrying out the responsibilities of the board
- Defining and communicating individual board responsibilities
- Hiring and assessing the CEO
- Establishing the board's role in resource development
- Organizing financial oversight
- Organizing program oversight
- Developing strategic leadership for future growth

An example of a highly successful board evaluation took place in a social service agency that focused on drug dependency issues. A new executive director suggested a board self-assessment as a first step in improving communication between board members and management. Data were collected through a review of background materials, individual in-depth interviews, and written, self-assessment questionnaires. These data pointed to a well-staffed board with a strong understanding of mission and vision, as well as a strong sense of commitment to the ministry of the organization. It was also clear that the board saw a need for greater communication and open discussion of issues facing the board and the organization, as well as a need for strengthening relationships both within the board and with external constituencies. The assessment expressed somewhat less satisfaction with implementation activities, such as implementing the vision statement, committee work, executive director evaluation, and risk management.

To address these needs, the board of directors agreed to restructure its committees to improve communication with all members regarding committee work and issue deliberation. They also agreed to establish goals and objectives for committee work, including benchmarks and ongoing evaluation criteria for board work. Additional efforts would be made to welcome and encourage participation from new board members. The board would also periodically review its roles and responsibilities in all areas of relating to external constituencies.

The assessment results led to the recommendation that the executive committee was playing too dominant a role and that the rest of the board wanted and needed to be more engaged. The board then clarified the role of the executive committee, restructured the board to eliminate several board committees, and refocused the board activity within three overarching committees. These changes redefined the roles and responsibilities of each board member, resulting in a greater utilization of each member's talents and abilities.

## Starting the CEO Evaluation Early

The successful CEO evaluation process should actually start before the CEO is hired. Based on its scan of the environment and current mission and vision for the future, the board needs to determine the desired CEO profile and the performance standards and benchmarks that should be required for the individual assuming the position. Then the recruitment process begins with a focus on finding a person who fits the profile and is capable of achieving the performance standards established. As a result, the stage is set for regular evaluation based on clear, mutually understood expectations. The board and CEO also need to understand that, as the organization changes, performance standards may need to be changed and that the board will identify these changes in partnership with the CEO, based on the current situation.

In the process of interviewing candidates for the CEO position, the search committee should clearly express priorities for the organization. Then, once hired, the CEO's initial goals need to be based on those priorities. Benchmarks or quantifiable steps toward achieving these goals need to be established at regular intervals, such as three, six, or nine months, leading up to an annual evaluation. These benchmarks are typically established through a consensus of the board and the CEO, with a clear understanding of how the benchmarks will be identified.

The CEO will be much more successful and effective if the individual in the position sees himself or herself as personally accountable for the goals that have been mutually established. The most successful evaluations are ones in which goals are established jointly by the board and the CEO. Knowing these goals early on, the CEO reports to the board on issues as they come up, not just at the time of formal evaluation. For instance, if a primary goal has been for the CEO to develop external relationships, but she finds that internal personnel management leaves little time for outside networking, she may bring this issue to the board. The board, in turn, may help to reassess priorities or reassign the personnel issues so that original priorities can be addressed.

## Establishing Good Communication

The key element in achieving successful board-CEO relationships is communication. If a CEO evaluation suggests that improvements need to be made, the very process of reporting and recommending creates a communication channel that wasn't there before the formal assessment process was initiated. The evaluation process should create an atmosphere for focused, direct communication on a regular basis between the board and the person held accountable for the day-to-day operation and implementation of the plan. With the evaluation process, the potential for meaningful, productive communication is greatly enhanced. If the CEO and board are unable to establish mutually acceptable goals and benchmarks, there is probably a serious communication problem between the board and CEO that needs to be addressed. Organizations face dangerous situations when conflicts or differences in expectations are identified and not resolved.

For example, a prominent theological school was failing financially and had declining enrollment. The board believed that quality issues were involved and that new financial resource options needed to be explored. Even though the current president had been in place for some time and the board was generally pleased with his performance over the long term, the board decided it needed to go beyond its usual brief evaluation of the president and conduct a more extensive and targeted evaluation. A small board committee, headed by a corporate human resources specialist, was appointed to carry out this important leadership evaluation. As a result of that evaluation, it was determined that, although the president had been effective at the beginning of his term, he was not prepared to lead the organization through the transformation process, which was essential if the school was going to survive. In a sensitive and appropriate manner, the board developed an exit plan for the current president and recruited a new CEO who had the personality and experience to lead the organization into the future. The transition to new leadership went smoothly, and the new president led the organization through significant program changes and recommended a shift in resource mix. The result is a school that is successful and thriving today.

## Identifying Disparities Between Board and CEO

If the CEO starts moving the organization down a path that differs from the board's vision, that variance will be quickly identified during an evaluation process. An increasing disparity between what the board expects and what is actually happening demands resolution in order to get the organization back on track. Ongoing evaluation through the review of established benchmarks will keep the gap between the CEO and the board from getting too wide. When the gap gets too wide, the CEO's job may be at stake or the board is in danger of losing its position as leader of the organization.

The board needs to maintain its position as overall policy- and direction-setter of the organization. A passive, nonresponding, nonassessing board can end up quickly having a CEO take the organization in a direction that it did not anticipate, did not want, and will not stand for when backed against the wall. Likewise, CEOs who find great disparity between what their boards expect and what, from their perspective, really needs to happen in the organization will not stay in their positions for long if their boards are not receptive to a changed direction. All too frequently, organizations lose talented CEOs because of misplaced or miscommunicated expectations.

This kind of unfortunate scenario is unlikely in a situation where a board and CEO have been clearly communicating and assessing progress all along. The successful evaluation process starts the day the CEO is hired, or even sooner, when expectations are set up on both sides. It's not necessary to wait a year to evaluate. The best evaluation processes are composed of regular, frequent, evaluative conversations with an annual, formal review.

## Handling CEO Evaluation Carefully

The CEO evaluation team could be composed of one individual, either the board chair or another designated person on the board, or several individuals, including the board chair and a human resource specialist or experienced organization leader who may be on the board. Sometimes in a small organization the board's executive committee serves as the evaluation team. As with board evaluations, there are a variety of assessment tools available, although CEO assessments are sometimes developed by boards based on their specific expectations.

Whatever characteristics the evaluation team establishes as goals for a new CEO and whatever evaluation tool is used, there are some basic characteristics that almost every board should look for in its prospective CEO during the evaluation process:

- Belief in the organization and a deep desire to move the organization forward to achieve its mission

- A clear understanding that the CEO has been hired by the board and is accountable to the board

- A willingness to work on a team and not autocratically, including a desire to work with other staff members and the board to create a real sense of working together

# Evaluating an In-Place CEO

When the evaluation process has not been initiated at the time of hiring or early during a CEO's tenure, it is more challenging to establish an effective evaluation process. Midstream creation of an evaluation process becomes especially difficult if the CEO's performance is not meeting the expectations of the board. Sometimes, when evaluation does not take place regularly, the board and CEO may find their roles reversed, with the CEO acting as head of both policy and operations while the board has become an advisory group to the CEO. This scenario is common in situations where the CEO has been very successful over a long period of time while the board has gradually assumed a passive role. The board attitude may be, "It's all going well, so why should we interfere?"

In either situation—whether the CEO has been successful or not—it is dangerous to forego the evaluation process. Without CEO (and board) evaluation, an organization can too easily veer off track, away from its mission and vision. With evaluation, even the most successful organizations can find renewed energy and purpose in the focus of their activities. Even the most effective CEOs can benefit (and their organizations can benefit) from a close review of work accomplished and goals set for the future.

Such an evaluation process can begin with the CEO and board chair reviewing strategic plans and setting CEO priorities, objectives, performance standards, and a plan for ongoing, regular evaluation. The CEO can state what he or she needs from the board chair and vice versa.

If performance evaluations are presented as opportunities for the mutual growth and development of both the CEO and the organization, the CEO will usually be receptive and understand that the focus is not criticism but improved communication and more focused strategic direction. The emphasis during the evaluation should be interactive, with both the CEO and the board presenting concerns and observations. The result will be a stronger organization that is more in tune with its mission and strategies for the future.

## Considering an Organizational Assessment

Fully engaged boards also need to be involved in organizational assessment. When anticipating change, boards need to look closely at their organizational structure, processes, and services, especially as they relate to emerging opportunities and issues. An organizational assessment can start with customer groups that can be asked their views concerning the organization's ability to provide current services. An organization also typically assesses itself as it relates to its capabilities, including its human resource capabilities, information systems, knowledge management capabilities, financial resources, and competencies related to possible directions.

Whatever tool is used, it is important to look at the elements essential for growth and transformation. In addition to assessing leadership at both the management and board levels, the marketplace currently being served needs to be researched and understood. Potential markets also need to be examined in light of future services. The ability to communicate throughout the organization and the marketplace should be assessed. The human resources and management structures should be reviewed. Financial models and the organization's ability to meet budgetary goals must be studied.

In a time of change, it is also important to look at the organization's ability to develop new programs and new strategies related to resources. How does the organization educate itself, and how are the results of learning and training filtered back into the organization? How effective is the organization in marketing and providing services? How is it delivering services into the marketplace?

An organizational assessment can take place as part of a board and management assessment, perhaps with the support of board-initiated action teams that are each assigned a specific area for review. As an example, the board of a very large, multifaceted grant-making organization with a focus on enterprise decided it needed an organizational assessment as the organization prepared to make major program and resource changes. A task force led by a board member was assigned the task of managing this assessment, which began in

the upper-management area and then moved to the marketplace—
to the customer who was receiving services. Members of the organization and constituents were asked in focus groups how they
perceived the organization and how they saw it moving into the future. That information was then taken back to senior management
for planning. The resulting proposal was presented to the board during a retreat, and the board then reviewed and approved, with
minor revisions, a revised mission, vision, and values statement in
preparation for major new initiatives throughout the organization.

In another situation, a system of colleges and universities was assessed by an outside consulting group. Although the education being
delivered was of high quality, the consultants recognized a need
throughout the system for strengthening in terms of delivery of education and marketing their programs. The consultants recommended
a stronger collaboration among the institutions, particularly as it related to marketing. The result was that the organization formed a
new corporation, with new brand identity goals. The new organization launched a substantial capitalization program to implement
new information and delivery systems that were unified and created
significant efficiencies for the organization. All this grew out of a
major organizational assessment.

Assessment and evaluation, whether the target is the CEO, the
board, or the organization itself, can be a positive, energizing experience for everyone involved if it is approached objectively and
with the good of the public trust as its primary goal. Most important, evaluation is an essential step that gives an organization the
knowledge and direction it needs to embark on a successful process
of change.

## Questions for Reflection

What kinds of performance evaluations does your board use now to assess your CEO? To assess the board itself? To assess the organization? Do you think this evaluation process could be improved?

Has it been more than two years since your board has conducted a formal evaluation process—of the CEO, of the organization, of the board?

Does your CEO seem to be moving in a different direction from your board? If so, what steps can you take so that the board and CEO start moving in the same direction?

When hiring a new CEO, are the board's expectations clearly stated up-front? Is an evaluation process in place up-front?

*Chapter Eight*

# A Final Word

## The Future of Board Leadership

The future changes every day!
*Old Iowa farm quote*

As the board goes, so goes the organization.
*Author's maxim*

In this chapter, the reader will learn how boards and their organizations are changing for the future and what will be expected of fully engaged board members.

George is a member of a college board of directors; however, he is temporarily residing in a country outside the United States. This has not caused any interruption in his board membership because he is able to use advanced technology to perform virtually all his board tasks. He sits at his computer and accesses a restricted forum for board members on the college's Web site, reads briefs, and reviews an agenda for an upcoming committee meeting. He has just attended a crucial executive committee meeting via a telephone conference where key decisions were made. Once a year, George attends a three-day retreat on campus. Other than that, he is able to conduct all his board business using the telephone and computer.

Jane has served a social service organization in a variety of volunteer capacities over a period of more than ten years. Early in her involvement with the agency, she served on the board of directors, and she has just joined the board again after being involved in a variety of hands-on committee projects. Her second experience on the board is very different from her first. The twelve-member board is now half the size of the earlier board and communicates regularly via e-mail and phone. Jane lives in a small Minnesota town, and an early-morning executive committee meeting has been scheduled on a day when the temperature is below zero; however, the meeting takes place via a telephone conference call. Not only does Jane avoid driving in bad weather, she saves the time it would take commuting to and from meetings. The meeting agenda involved a feasibility study for a specific project within the organization's strategic plan that needs capital funding. Because of her history with the organization, Jane is fully capable of making decisions without face-to-face discussion.

Throughout this book, we've been emphasizing the point that for many years into the future, most nonprofit organizations will continue to be in a constant state of change. This creates a unique and challenging climate for a board of directors charged with overseeing a public trust. As a result, boards will have to be much more intensely engaged in their roles, particularly as they set policies and develop plans to accommodate fast-paced and dramatic change. The engagement model for board governance being proposed in this book reflects a board that is more deeply involved than ever before.

As we progress into this new century, board members will undoubtedly rediscover what it means to be a public trust—in control of policy, plans, and mission for a community. In the past and into the present, too many nonprofits have lost their way when it comes to setting policy and overseeing their organizations. The result is boards that are not in control of the public trust. This problem is evident across the wide spectrum of nonprofit organizations—from colleges to health care organizations, from church-related groups to social service agencies and cultural entities.

Too often an organization's employees are inappropriately moving beyond their day-to-day, operational activities and are actually setting policy. When this happens, boards serve merely as reaction groups. Fortunately, because of the critical issues and high risks they are facing, many fully engaged boards are recognizing that they will have to assume their priority role of setting policy and establishing plans and mission.

Boards are also recognizing the importance of having continuous discussions around mission, organizational direction, and strategy as these elements relate to priority constituents or markets they have targeted to serve. The emphasis here is on *continuous*. In the past, boards have had these kinds of discussions occasionally or, worse yet, these discussions have occurred at the staff level and not at the board level. Too often boards have focused on operational details and not on the big ideas—the vision for the organization.

The engagement model of board governance will have increasing importance for nonprofit organizations operating in this new century. When board members think about their agendas for the future, they will need to ask these key questions:

Is the agenda appropriate for a transforming organization?

Are all the organization's bases covered?

Are the board's priorities straight?

Are board members fully engaged with the CEO and senior management in planning and resource development as well as in setting policy?

Boards that follow the engagement model described in this book will find that it instills commitment, increased motivation, and excitement among board members. Engaged board members are still very involved in policy setting, but they go way beyond this narrow role. They are involved in a continual planning process and are developing key relationships among targeted groups of constituents. They are deeply involved in recruiting and evaluating leaders at the board and management levels—leaders who can take their organizations through dynamic transformation. And they are exploring and then leading their organizations to establish a new mix of resources that will allow them to grow and serve their changing missions and marketplaces.

## Preparing for Change

Boards in the future (and this is happening to many boards right now) will transform themselves as their organizations are also transforming. Boards are changing in the following key ways:

• *Technology is driving boards toward new, more efficient ways of delivering and marketing services and also of operating and communicating internally.* These changes will raise all kinds of questions about policies as they relate to serving in a technological age. For instance, the availability of lower-cost medicines from other countries via the Internet generates key policy questions about whether hospitals should be purchasing these drugs in order to keep sky-rocketing health care costs down.

Technology will play a significant role in the way boards operate in the future. Board meetings will take place via a mixture of face-to-face and technology-supported meetings. Some meetings will take place in the form of "your time" on-line discussions in which board members will be able to access and exchange information according to their own time schedules. Other meetings will be "real time" discussions through video conferencing or electronic Web sites. Preparation for meetings will frequently take place through organizational Web sites where agendas can be developed and reviewed, questions raised, and background material communicated. Evaluations of the board and CEO will also be developed through electronic communication. Board members, committee members, and management leadership will be able to easily dialogue with each other electronically.

Many more boards today are studying, reviewing, and making decisions electronically, which improves the efficiencies and communication between an organization's board members and management. Boards will have their own Web sites where they will be able to review minutes and committee reports, staying in closer touch than ever before with their organizations and the directions they are moving.

Board members will undoubtedly find that technology increases the level and intensity of their board participation. This move toward increased technology use means that board members will need to become up to speed technologically. Some boards are even offering their board members computer training programs and access to computers.

• *Boards will be facing the inevitable elimination of programs within their organizations.* Missions, visions, and values that have been cherished for decades may need to be discarded and replaced, resulting in program and service endings that may be very difficult to accept. For example, a university may decide to eliminate several major programs that are no longer relevant to students; however, what happens to the tenured faculty members who teach in these programs? Teachers unions have already taken universities to court over similar issues.

In some instances, boards will need to decide whether the entire organization should be abandoned and service stopped. As figures earlier in this book indicated, many nonprofits start annually but many more cease operations. The reasons are varied. Perhaps the problem or need that was the organization's raison d'être no longer exists and the service provided is no longer needed, or perhaps the organization has no resources to continue its programming.

• *Where the organization will go in the future will become the overriding issue facing boards.* Although in the past boards were content to establish and monitor policies around current missions and programs, significant transformation will thrust boards into major decision-making modes as far as the future of their organizations. For example, should a floundering nonprofit consider merging all or part of its organization with a for-profit entity? There are many examples of this already happening, particularly in the health care arena where frequently the only way a hospital can survive is to merge and become part of a for-profit organization. There are also examples of for-profit hospitals selling pieces of their organizations to nonprofits. The variations are myriad, and boards will be faced with the need to make difficult decisions related to these kinds of options.

• *In order to respond to the rapid pace of change and the volatility of markets, boards will be smaller but more dynamic.* Organizations will find that there are other meaningful ways to involve people in their organizations than as board members. People can effectively connect to organizations through their specific talents, including involvement in fundraising. These smaller boards will be able to operate more efficiently and intensely in a fast-paced, changing environment.

• *Boards will need to be more resourceful and their memberships more diverse.* Organizations will have to recruit top talent for their boards and leadership positions. Board members will be expected to bring in key relationships and generate respect in the marketplace. Board members will have to be team players, with the ability to work effectively in a group while bringing more than one key attribute to the board. For instance, having wealth will no longer be enough. Boards need members with multiple skills and connections—members who can be valuable resources for their organizations.

Inclusiveness will be a strong trend in the future, as boards realize the value of diverse members from a range of age groups, professions, ethnic groups, and value systems. Boards will face the question, How do we build agendas and coalitions when our members represent such a wide range of generational, ethnic, cultural, business, and social groups? Board members will need to focus more on team building, working together, and understanding one another.

• *Board members will need to make intense commitments to their board responsibilities.* However, because of technology these commitments will not necessarily mean more on-site involvement or more time devoted to board meetings. Instead, time spent on board activities will be more focused and demand more energy and skill. There are emerging examples of small, dynamic boards with this intense commitment—boards that are much stronger than larger boards with cumbersome meeting schedules. This intense commitment may result in board members cycling in and out appropriately, depending on their available time to be fully engaged as they serve on the board. Board commitments may be shorter but more concentrated.

• *Boards will need to look hard at their organization's resources and explore different resource solutions or a different balance of existing resources.* Boards will need to build relationships with newly developing groups of donors. New collaborative relationships and alliances will demand new policies related to resources. Boards may need to partner to ensure that they have the resources to accomplish their plans. Having the funds and people to implement plans is as important an agenda item as making the plans themselves. Boards may have good plans and ideas but neglect to put in place the resources necessary for accomplishing these goals. Boards need to focus on matching ideas with resource plans that relate to people, systems, and money. Boards that are not looking at resource plans are not fully engaged and may actually be considered negligent. They may never play the key roles they should be playing in moving their organizations forward.

## Becoming Aware of Developing Themes

Several significant themes are starting to repeat themselves as they emerge in the environment in which nonprofit organizations operate. These themes are so strong and so all-encompassing that they will dramatically affect the way nonprofits need to operate within their environments. Boards of directors need to raise their consciousness about these realities and start devising plans that acknowledge and address these issues. Some of these themes are discussed in the sections that follow.

## The Relationship Age

Relationships are a key focus of a nonprofit's mission and goals, particularly during the transformation process; however, the nature of relationships is shifting in dramatic ways.

**From Your Place to Mine.** Shifts are taking place in which relationships and services come to the consumer; the consumer doesn't have to go to the services. For instance, instead of shopping in stores, more and more people are shopping at home through catalogues and computers, which allow consumers to make purchases on-line. For some time, health care has been moving from inpatient stays to day surgery and home care. Education is taking place on-line and via long-distance conferencing. Social service agencies are providing services on the customer's sites rather than on their own sites. Nonprofits that are open to shifting the place where service is provided have a much better chance of success than those that aren't considering this option. Technology enhances opportunities for connectiveness, but it also is starting to close the door on traditional modes of providing service.

**From Access to Privacy.** Advancing technology has also limited accessibility in a variety of ways. When most people lived in traditional neighborhoods, they were accessible. Now some people have moved to planned communities that protect their privacy with gates, locks, and heightened security. As a result, they are not nearly as accessible to their neighbors and others who want to connect with them. Even cell phones have voice mail with caller-ID systems that tell who is calling, so it is possible to screen callers. E-mail allows message recipients to choose whose messages we read and whose are deleted or ignored. Many people have several different e-mail addresses for different groups of contacts. Consequently, despite all the media attention to privacy issues, today it is actually becoming much easier for individuals to protect their privacy if they choose to do so. As a result, nonprofit organizations may not be able to access their constituents in the traditional ways. This overwhelming trend toward privacy puts the individual more in control of making choices related to various constituency groups. People can get completely lost if they choose to do so. So nonprofits will need to develop new strategies for finding and communicating with their target constituency groups.

*From a Single Community to Myriad Options.* People are so inundated with messages and have so many opportunities for response that they need to filter their messages. People today live in multiple communities enhanced by technology—virtual communities, work communities, volunteer communities, health communities, family communities—and they are all sending messages. Options for involvement and response are greater than at any time in the history of mankind. Some busy, involved people receive hundreds of e-mail messages a day and just as many voice mail messages. The competition for time, talents, and resources is much more intense today than it was even five years ago. The challenge is immense for nonprofits facing this environment as they try to reach their supporters and constituents. This challenge will only increase in the years to come.

*From In-Depth Relationships to Multiple Touch-Points.* All these factors—the focus on privacy, myriad options, and technology—combine to create many more relationship opportunities for each individual; however, the scope and depth of these relationships are compromised by their very quantity. Most people today do not spend as much quality time in any of their relationships. In fact, they have become so accustomed to fast-paced communication in their relationships that they have little time for the in-depth discussion and interchange that allow true understanding of the other party. This is a dangerous trend for organizations that want to build deeper relationships on their boards, within their organizations, and with their supporters and constituents. So nonprofits are not only facing the question of how to develop relationships but how to make them meaningful.

## A Boundaryless Environment

Organizations going through significant change are also seeing major shifts in channels of social, economic, and institutional power, including the following:

*From Face-to-Face to Electronically Mediated Interaction.* What happens when products and services can be purchased from anywhere in the world on-line? When services can be accessed across the globe? When pharmaceuticals can be prescribed on-line and delivered all over the world? When students can take courses and even earn degrees without ever leaving their homes? And when all this can happen almost instantaneously? Through technology, that capability is here today, and, as more individuals and organizations embrace these opportunities, the impact on nonprofits will be immense. Missions, policies, plans, and market designations will need to be changed as organizations embark on this whole new boundaryless paradigm.

*From Country to Global and Regional Power.* Traditional boundaries across the country and the world are starting to break down. This fragmentation is resulting in a repackaging of populations into regional communities. Markets are being defined in different ways, not so much as states or countries but as consumer groups that behave in a similar fashion and reside in proximity to each other. New forms of regional government and economies are following these lines, and, therefore, nonprofit organizations serving these new regions are beginning to realign their operating structures to reflect new relationships that are not restricted to the old borders.

For example, Goodwill Industries of Southeastern Wisconsin was once Goodwill Industries of Milwaukee and has recently expanded to bring northwestern Illinois into its fold, creating a Great Lakes region as its marketplace. The border between Wisconsin and Illinois, once the logical line of division, has become meaningless. These changes have meant a reorganization of Goodwill's board to make it more regional and have resulted in substantial changes in bylaws, policies, and marketing strategies. So as this boundaryless paradigm continues to evolve, nonprofit boards of directors will need to look closely at their missions and policies and redefine them for the new marketplaces being established.

*From Hierarchies to Networks and Alliances.* Organizations that were once organized from the top down are now realizing that this archaic structure needs to be replaced by a more horizontal organizational structure that emphasizes alliances, interconnected networks, and collaborations. The human resources impact on organizations is immense.

### A Changing Public Policy and Funding Environment

A major shift is taking place in our society away from the concept of entitlement. We see it related to welfare, where very few groups are considered entitled to anything. Individuals are expected to work in exchange for what they are given. In higher education, for instance, tuition has typically been significantly discounted, resulting in students not paying the actual cost of their education. Boards of colleges and universities are now starting to ask what the real cost of a student's education is and are then looking closely at how those costs should be covered. They are asking, How much should a student pay for his or her education, and how much should be covered through a combination of loans, work, financial aid, and philanthropy? Very few students are deemed entitled to a completely free education.

In health care, this trend has been evolving for some time, as health care providers realized that uncompensated care was destabilizing their institutions. This realization has presented a real dilemma for hospital boards that still want to meet their missions of providing health care to all who need it but know their institutions cannot survive if other resource solutions are not in place.

In addition, nonprofits are no longer the only providers of a range of services that were once solely their domain. They find themselves competing with for-profits in all kinds of arenas that for-profits didn't touch a decade ago, such as managing schools, managing prisons, and providing health care. Nonprofits themselves are no longer automatically entitled to receive these contracts and are operating in a very competitive environment. This creates all kinds of policy questions for nonprofit boards of directors as they struggle with their positioning in the marketplace. Boards must ask, In this environment, what are the advantages of being a nonprofit versus a for-profit entity?

Nonprofits are also discovering that they are not automatically entitled to a totally tax-free environment. As they pursue a variety of enterprises and other revenue-generating solutions, they must be very careful to ensure that their ventures still support their missions in order for them to remain tax-free. Nonprofit organizations are finding themselves much more closely scrutinized by local, state, and federal governments that may be questioning their nonprofit status. For instance, in some cities for-profit health clubs are asking why YMCA health facilities are not taxed. These for-profit clubs suggest that the YMCAs have an unfair competitive advantage because of their non-taxable status.

## Shifts in Revenue Sources

Several dynamic shifts taking place in nonprofit revenue sources are discussed in the sections that follow.

*Growth in the Assets of Community and Other Foundations.* One of the fastest-growing sources of gifts and grants sought by nonprofits are community foundations throughout the country. The healthy economy during the last decade has resulted in tremendous philanthropic support for many of these foundations, leaving some of them in the unique situation of having more money than their current systems of distribution are prepared to handle. Some of these foundations, in an effort to be good stewards of their funds, have even temporarily stopped increasing their giving programs as they review and transform their policies and plans. Ironically, this situation could have a detrimental effect on some nonprofits that will not receive the increased gifts they had anticipated.

*Shifts in Corporate Funding from Philanthropy to Marketing Partnerships.* Boards are also noticing a shift in corporate funding from straight philanthropy to the establishment of marketing partnerships. Corporations are developing a strong self-interest when it comes to their giving programs. As mentioned earlier, younger donors in particular are not so much philanthropists as focused investors who expect their gifts to generate visible results that directly benefit their businesses and even themselves as individuals. We are seeing the evolvement of a self-interest investment process versus the traditional philanthropic approach of giving and feeling good about it, while not ever seeing any direct impact. Boards will need to consider what partnerships could be developed and how they can attract these new kinds of corporate donors whose attitudes toward giving have shifted dramatically.

*Publicly Funded Agencies Competing for Private Gifts.* Publicly funded agencies and institutions have decided that private gifting and grants are fair game, and they are going after this lucrative source of revenue with intensity and a high level of sophistication. As a result, we have public schools setting up private foundations to compete with private nonprofit schools. Higher education has recognized the value of private endowments and foundations for some time. Public libraries are setting up private foundations to do the same thing. Even cities or their special interest departments are setting up private foundations. County and state parks are creating private foundations through friends' groups that are seeking corporate and private donations. We even have governments establishing private foundations for a variety of public-interest initiatives. As a result, boards of directors of nonprofits are finding themselves in the unique position of needing to compete intensely in ways they never experienced before. Frequently, these boards do not have the expertise to compete as effectively as for-profit entities in this new marketplace environment.

## A Consumer-Oriented Marketplace

Major shifts are taking place—from an emphasis on customer transactions to customer loyalty. Organizations are developing lifelong, rather than one-time, relationships with their customers. The needs and desires of the customer must be foremost in the minds of those providing services and products. Wise organizations are focusing on interactive relationships where they are always testing the needs and desires of their constituents. Building loyalty is a primary goal. This is all taking place against the backdrop of a society that is transactional and has devalued loyalty. Thus when an organization places an emphasis on developing loyalty among customers, it needs to be perceived as providing long-term value. And in that process, the organization will build loyalty in an environment where loyalty is disintegrating. Nonprofit organizations must revise their policies and plans to focus on developing committed, extended relationships with loyal constituents.

## Anticipating Changes in Board Membership

Organizations will find increasing ways to tap into the skills and experience their board members offer. Board members may act in a variety of roles—as recruiters, evaluators, teachers, consultants for special projects, public relations specialists, or problem solvers. Increasingly, board members will become spokespersons for their organizations and will have major relationship-building responsibilities. They will frequently join forces with their organization's management in presenting the organization to constituents, the media, and supporters.

Alternative structures for board membership are being explored. For instance, the National Center for Nonprofit Boards and the Hauser Center at Harvard are looking at models in which senior staff comprise a significant portion of the board. This is a similar approach to corporations that have "inside" and "outside" directors on their corporate boards. There are obvious advantages to having more insiders, who are already fully engaged in an organization's operations, on boards of directors. There are also obvious risks that need to be considered.

Some nonprofit boards have started to follow the examples of their corporate counterparts and compensate their board members or at least cover travel expenses, although in some states there are regulations regarding the extent of nonprofit board compensation. In some organizations today, we see dysfunction that is primarily the result of volunteer board membership. Volunteers may not have the time, the commitment, the expertise, or the accountability to lead transforming organizations successfully into the future. Many large, national nonprofit boards today are already paying their members stipends and covering their expenses.

The traditional role of board members as financial supporters and fundraisers will intensify, along with an increased emphasis on planning and resource development. Board members who are effective will be thinking hard with their CEOs about changed missions and future directions for their organizations. The result will be high-level problem-solving, leading to new directional initiatives. As organizations go through transformation and rapid change, board members will frequently be the historians who give the organization a sense of the past as a foundation for the future. As board members become more deeply involved in organizations, they will need increased management support.

Nonprofit board members and organization leaders are embarking on an exciting time to be involved in nonprofit organizations, but it is not a time for the faint of heart. Nonprofit leaders must be willing to become fully engaged in the process of serving their organizations, committing and working at the peak of their performance capabilities. In return, they will find their board experiences to be immensely productive and rewarding, and their organizations will reap tremendous benefits.

---

### Questions for Reflection

What new agenda items mentioned in this chapter has your board started to address? Which ones do you feel your board should address?

Is your board prepared to face the inevitable changes that will confront all boards in the future? What can you do to become more prepared?

Does your organization have one or more board members who live in another area of the country or travel extensively? Do you sometimes have difficulty reaching the CEO or other board members? Does the CEO have trouble reaching you?

Is your organization conducting meetings the same way it did five years ago? How can your board start using new technologies effectively to make board tasks more efficient?

How do you think your role as a board member will change in the future? Should you start embracing some of these changes now?

What benefits do you see for your organization, your board, and yourself as the changes suggested in this chapter become reality?

# Checklist for Engaged Boards

The following questions are organized in the seven key areas of board responsibility emphasized in the engagement model of board governance. If your board can answer yes to most of these questions, then your board is probably already well on its way to embracing the engagement model. If you cannot answer yes to most of these questions, then you may need to consider whether the engagement model might be a more effective approach to leadership for your board to consider, particularly if you anticipate significant change taking place in your organization in the near future.

### Recruitment

Do your board and CEO work together to set leadership responsibilities, goals, and objectives?

Do you have specific, measurable performance objectives in place for your CEO and your board members?

Do you have plans in place for ongoing board member recruitment and development? Do you have a committee looking at this process on an ongoing basis?

Do you feel that your board is diverse enough to fully understand the constituency you serve?

### Preparation

Do your board and CEO work together to define the format for meeting preparations, orientation, communication strategies, and tools?

Is the importance of preparation emphasized in your board's recruitment process?

Does your board have a preparation plan, and is it reviewed regularly for effectiveness?

Do your board members spend less time preparing for board meetings than they spend attending board meetings?

### Policy

Do your board and CEO continuously review established policies in light of rapidly changing environmental factors?

Has your board established appropriate policies in marketing, services, human resources, and financial resources?

Does your board include the CEO in discussions about policies as they affect operations?

Do you feel uncomfortable bringing new issues or possible policy conflicts to the board for discussion and action?

### Planning

Are your board and CEO regularly engaged in a review of planning process design?

Has your board recently reviewed its mission and vision, as well as its underlying values?

Has your board discussed trend data, benchmarks, or leading indicators for your organization in the last six months?

Does your board understand the environment in which its organization is operating?

### Positioning and Public Relations

How long has it been since your board surveyed constituents and determined your organization's position within the marketplace?

Has your board developed a case statement that reflects the main focus of your positioning efforts?

Does your board prioritize the development of relationships? Do board members understand their responsibility in bringing new relationships to the organization?

Do you have a system (MIS) for managing your database of contacts and relationships? If so, is it up to date and organized to be helpful to your marketing efforts?

### Financial Resources

Has your board recently reviewed its current mix of resources? Has your board recently considered or implemented new resource solutions?

Have the words *enterprise* or *collaboration* been mentioned at any of your recent board meetings?

Do your board members understand how your organization's funds are being managed? Has your fund management approach been evaluated in the last year?

Do 100 percent of your board members contribute to the organization in significant ways, either monetarily or through bringing other major contributions into the organization?

### Performance Evaluation

Has your board conducted a formal evaluation process in the last two years—of the CEO, of the organization, and of the board?

When hiring a new CEO, are your board's expectations clearly stated up-front? Is an evaluation process in place up-front?

Do your board and CEO seem to be moving in the same direction and to have the same understanding of the organization's mission and objectives?

# Resources

## Governance

### Organizations

Association of Governing Boards of Colleges and Universities
1 Dupont Circle NW, Suite 400
Washington, DC 20036
(202) 296-8400
http://www.agb.org

The Century Foundation (formerly The Twentieth Century Fund)
41 East 70th Street
New York, NY 10021
(212) 535-4441
Fax: (212) 535-7534
http://www.tcp.org

National Center for Nonprofit Boards
2000 L Street NW, Suite 510
Washington, DC 20036
(202) 452-6262
http://www.ncnb.org

### Books

Abrahams, J. *The Mission Statement Book.* Berkeley, Calif.: Ten Speed Press, 1995.
Bennis, W. *Visionary Leadership: Creating a Compelling Sense of Direction for Your Organization.* San Francisco: Jossey-Bass, 1995.

Bryson, J. M. *Strategic Planning for Public and Nonprofit Organizations: A Guide to Strengthening and Sustaining Organizational Achievement.* San Francisco: Jossey-Bass, 1995.

Carver, J. *Boards That Make a Difference: A New Design for Leadership in Nonprofit and Public Organizations.* San Francisco: Jossey-Bass, 1997.

Carver, J., and Carver, M. M. *CarverGuide Series on Effective Board Governance.* San Francisco: Jossey Bass:
*Basic Principles of Policy Governance* (1996)
*Your Roles and Responsibilities as a Board Member* (1996)
*Three Steps to Fiduciary Responsibility* (1996)
*The Chairperson's Role as Servant-Leader to the Board* (1997)
*Planning Better Board Meetings* (1997)
*Creating a Mission That Makes a Difference* (1997)

Chait, R. P., Holland, T. P., and Taylor, B. E. *Improving the Performance of Governing Boards* (American Council on Education/Oryx Press Series on Higher Education). Westport, Conn.: Oryx Press, 1977.

Chait, R. P., Holland, T. P., and Taylor, B. E. *The Effective Board of Trustees.* New York: Macmillan, 1991.

DePree, M. *Leadership Is An Art.* Max Dell, 1989.

Drucker, P. F. *Lessons In Leadership: Facilitator's Guide.* San Francisco: Jossey-Bass, 1998.

Drucker, P. F. *Managing in a Time of Great Change.* New York: Truman Talley Books/Dutton, 1995.

Ellis, S. *The Board's Role in Effective Volunteer Involvement.* Washington, D.C.: National Center for Nonprofit Boards, 1995.

Frantzreb, A. C. *Not on This Board You Don't.* Chicago: Bonus Books, 1997.

Hammer, M. *Reengineering the Corporation: A Manifesto for Business Revolution.* New York: HarperCollins, 1993.

Hammer, M., and Stanton, S. A. *The Reengineering Revolution: A Handbook.* New York: HarperCollins, 1995.

Handy, C. *Beyond Certainty: The Changing Worlds of Organizations.* Boston: Harvard Business School Press, 1998.

Holland, T. P., and Blackmon, M. *Measuring Board Effectiveness.* Washington, D.C.: National Center for Nonprofit Boards, 2000.

Houle, C. O. *Governing Boards: Their Nature and Nurture.* San Francisco: Jossey-Bass, 1989.

Kennedy, D., Green, S. K., Hesselbein, F., and Drucker Foundation, P. F. *Action Dialogues: Meaningful Conversations to Accelerate Change* (Diversity Breakthrough! Strategic Action Series). San Francisco: Berrett-Koehler, 2000.

Kotter, J. P. *Leading Change.* Boston: Harvard Business School Press, 1996.

Miles, M. B. *Learning to Work in Groups.* New York: Teachers College, 1959.

Myers, J. H. *Segmentation and Positioning for Strategic Marketing Decisions.* Chicago: American Marketing Association, 1996.

Nanus, B. *Visionary Leadership*. San Francisco: Jossey-Bass, 1992.

*Nonprofit Governance Series*. Washington, D.C.: National Center for Nonprofit Boards:

*Board Assessment of the Chief Executive* (Nason), 1990

*The Chief Executive's Role in Developing the Nonprofit Board* (Axelrod), 1990

*The Nonprofit Board's Role in Risk Management* (Tremper-Babcock), 1990

*Board Passages: Three Key Stages in a Nonprofit Board's Life Cycle* (Mathiasen), 1991

*Creating and Renewing Advisory Boards: Strategies for Success* (Axelrod), 1991

*Planning Successful Board Retreats* (Bader), 1991

*Understanding Nonprofit Financial Statements* (Dalsimer), 1991

*Board Assessment of the Organization* (Szanton), 1992

*The Board's Role in Public Relations and Communications* (Fitzpatrick), 1992

*Bridging the Gap Between Nonprofit and For-Profit Board Members* (Lascell and Jensen), 1992

*The Role of the Board Chairperson* (Dorsey), 1992

*Smarter Board Meetings for Effective Nonprofit Governance* (Mueller), 1992

*Finding and Retaining Your Next Chief Executive* (Gilmore), 1993

*The Board's Role in Strategic Planning* (Park), 1996

*Ten Basic Responsibilities of Nonprofit Boards* (Ingram), 1996

*Fund Raising and the Nonprofit Board Member* (Howe), 1998

O'Connell, B. *The Board Members Book*. New York: The Foundation Center, 1993.

Oliver, C., and others. *The Policy Governance Fieldbook: Practical Lessons, Tips, and Tools from the Experience of Real-World Boards*. San Francisco: Jossey-Bass, 1999.

O'Toole, J. *Leading Change: The Argument for Values-Based Leadership*. San Francisco: Jossey-Bass, 1995.

Panas, J. *Boardroom Verities*. Chicago: Bonus Books, March, 1998.

Peters, T. J. *Thriving on Chaos: Handbook for a Management Revolution*. New York: Knopf, 1987.

Peters, T., Austin, N. K., and Peters, T. J. *A Passion for Excellence: The Leadership Difference*. New York: Warner Books, 1989.

Peters, T., and Townsend, R. *Excellence in the Organization*. New York: Simon & Schuster, 1995.

Royer, G. *School Board Leadership 2000: The Things Staff Didn't Tell You at Orientation*. Boston: Brockton Publishing, 1996.

Scribner, S. M. *BOARDS FROM HELL!* [http://www.thecuttingedge.com/Consult/S_Scribner/BoardsHell.htm].

Slesinger, L. H. *Self-Assessment for Nonprofit Governing Boards*. Washington, D.C.: National Center for Nonprofit Boards, 1995.

Smith, D. K. *Taking Charge of Change: Ten Principles for Managing People and Performance*. Reading, Mass.: Addison-Wesley, 1996.

Tyler, S. K. *Creating Caring and Capable Boards*. San Francisco: Jossey-Bass, 2000.

Wall, B., Solum, R., and Sobol, M. *The Visionary Leader: From Mission Statement to a Thriving Organization*. Rocklin, Calif.: Prima, 1992.

# Nonprofit

## Organizations

Association of Lutheran Development Executives
PO Box 930303
Verona, WI 53593
(800) 458-2363
Fax: (309) 664-2931
E-mail: staff@alde.org

The Chronicle of Philanthropy
1255 23rd Street NW
Washington, DC 20037
(202) 466-1200
http://www.philanthropy.com

Council on Foundations
1828 L Street, NW, Suite 300
Washington, DC 20036
(202) 466-6512
http://www.cof.org

Peter F. Drucker Foundation for Nonprofit Management
320 Park Avenue, 3rd Floor
New York, NY 10022
(212) 224-1174
Fax: (212) 224-2508
http://www.pfdf.org

The Foundation Center
79 Fifth Avenue
New York, NY 10003–3076
(212) 620-4230
Fax: (212) 691-1828
http://www.fdncenter.org


Growth Design Corporation
301 E. Reservoir Ave.
Milwaukee, WI 53212
(414) 224-0586
Fax: (414) 224-9371
http://www.growthdesign.com


The Internet Nonprofit Center
The Evergreen State Society
PO Box 20682
Seattle, WA 98102
http://www.nonprofits.org


National Center for Charitable Statistics
2100 M Street NW
Washington, DC 20037
(202) 261-5801
http://www.nccs.urban.org


National Charities Information Bureau
19 Union Square West
New York, NY 10003
(212) 929-6300
Fax: (212) 463-7083
http://give.org

National Society of Fund Raising Executives (NSFRE)
1101 King Street, Suite 700
Alexandria, VA 22314
(703) 684-0410
http://www.nsfre.org

Non-Profit Nuts & Bolts
Nuts & Bolts Publishing
4623 Tiffany Woods Circle
Oviedo, FL 32765
(407) 677-6564
Fax: (407) 677-5645
http://www.nutsbolts.com

The Non-Profit Times
240 Cedar Knolls Road, Suite 318
Cedar Knolls, NJ 07927
(973) 734-1700
Fax: (973) 734-1777
http://www.nptimes.com

## Books

Allison, M., and Kaye, J. *Strategic Planning for Nonprofit Organizations: A Practical Guide and Workbook*. New York: Wiley, 1997.

Barry, B. *Strategic Planning Workbook for Nonprofit Organizations, Revised and Updated*. St. Paul, Minn.: Amherst H. Wilder Foundation, 1997.

Coy, J. F. *Integrating Corporate Community Involvement for Added Value: Trends and Case Studies*. New York: Council on Foundations, 1996.

Eadie, D. C. *Changing by Design: A Practical Approach to Leading Innovation in Nonprofit Organizations*. San Francisco: Jossey-Bass, 1997.

*Giving and Volunteering in the United States*. Washington, D.C.: INDEPENDENT SECTOR, 1999.

Grace, K. S. *Beyond Fundraising: New Strategies for Nonprofit Innovation and Management*. New York: Wiley, 1997.

Herman, R. D. *The Jossey-Bass Handbook of Nonprofit Leadership and Management*. San Francisco: Jossey-Bass, 1994.

Hodgkinson, V. A., Weitzman, M. S., Toppe, C. M., and Noga, S. M. *Nonprofit Almanac: Dimensions of the Independent Sector, 1992–1993.* San Francisco: Jossey-Bass, 1992.

Howe, F. *The Board Member's Guide to Fund Raising.* San Francisco: Jossey-Bass, 1991.

Kaplan, A. E. *Giving USA: The Annual Report of Philanthropy.* New York: American Association of Fund Raising Counsel, Trust for Philanthropy, 1999.

Lindahl, W. E. *Strategic Planning for Fund Raising.* San Francisco: Jossey-Bass, 1992.

Lohmann, R. A. (ed.). *Nonprofit Management & Leadership.* San Francisco: Jossey-Bass (quarterly).

Olenick, A. J., and Olenick, P. R. *A Nonprofit Organization Operating Manual: Planning for Survival and Growth.* New York: The Foundation Center, July, 1991.

# References

AAFRC Trust for Philanthropy. *Giving USA 2000: The Annual Report on Philanthropy*. Indianapolis: AAFRC Trust for Philanthropy, 2000, pp. 18–19.

Abrahams, J. *The Mission Statement Book: 301 Corporate Mission Statements from America's Top Companies*. Berkeley, Calif.: Ten Speed Press, 1995, p. 38.

Abramson, A. J., and Salamon, L. M. *Nonprofit Sector and the Federal Budget: Update as of September 1997*. Washington, D.C.: INDEPENDENT SECTOR, Sept. 1997.

Basinger, J. "College Trustees Often Fumble Presidential Transitions Reports Feds." [http://www.chronicle.com], July 23, 2001.

Carver, J., and Carver, M. M. *Basic Principles of Policy Governance*. San Francisco: Jossey-Bass, 1996a.

Carver, J., and Carver, M. M. *Your Roles and Responsibilities as a Board Member* (Carverguide Series on Effective Board Governance, no. 2). San Francisco: Jossey-Bass, 1996b.

"Diversity Increases Among Presidents." *Chronicle of Higher Education*, Sept. 15, 2000, p. A31.

Dobrzynski, J. "Executive Tests Now Plumb New Depths of the Job Seeker." *New York Times*, Sept. 2, 1996, S1, p. 1.

Drucker, P. *Managing in a Time of Change*. New York: Truman Talley Books, 1995, p. 39.

Emerson, J. *New Social Entrepreneurs: The Success, Challenge, and Lessons of Non-Profit Enterprise Creation*. San Francisco: The Roberts Foundation, 1996.

Ghering, J. "College Board Reports 'Modest' Increases in Tuition." [http://www.edweek.org], Oct. 25, 2000.

Gladwell, M. *The Tipping Point*. New York: Little, Brown, 2000.

Greenfeld, K. T. "A New Way of Giving." *Time*, July 24, 2000, p. 49.

Hammer, M., and Champy, J. *Reengineering the Corporation*. New York: Harper-Collins, 1993.

Hodgkinson, V. A., and Weitzman, M. S. *Nonprofit Almanac: Dimensions of the Independent Sector 1996–1997*. San Francisco: Jossey-Bass, 1996.

Internal Revenue Service. *Statistics on Income Bulletin*. Washington, D.C.: U.S. Government Printing Office. Internal Revenue Service, Spring 2000.

Kanter, R. M. "The Emerging Skills of Change Leaders." *Ivey Business Journal*. May-June 2000, 64(5), 32.

Kotter, J. *Leading Change*. Boston: Harvard Business School Press, 1996.

Lewis, J. *Partnerships for Profit: Structuring and Managing Strategic Alliances*. New York: Free Press, 1990.

Lipman-Blumen, J. *The Connective Edge: Leading in an Interdependent World*. San Francisco: Jossey-Bass, 1996.

Marchetti, D. "Charities Face Mounting Challenges in Hiring and Retaining Executives." *The Chronicle of Philanthropy—Managing Nonprofit Groups*, June 3, 1999.

Mattessich, P., and Monsey, B. *Collaboration: What Makes It Work*. St. Paul, Minn.: Amherst H. Wilder Foundation, 1992.

Moss, K. R. "The Emerging Skills of Change Leaders." *Ivey Business Journal*. May-June 2000, 64(5), 32.

National Center for Nonprofit Boards and Stanford University. *The Nonprofit Governance Index*. Washington, D.C.: National Center for Nonprofit Boards and Stanford University, 2000.

Pappas, A. T. *Reengineering Your Nonprofit Organization: A Guide to Strategic Transformation*. New York: Wiley, 1995.

Prince, R. A., and File, K. M. *The Seven Faces of Philanthropy: A New Approach to Cultivating Major Donors*. San Francisco: Jossey-Bass, 1994.

Reisberg, L. "Average Tuition and Fees at Colleges Rose Less Than 5% This Year." *Chronicle of Higher Education: Students*, Oct. 15, 1999.

Ries, A., and Trout, J. *Positioning: The Battle for Your Mind*. New York: McGraw-Hill, 2001.

Stanley, T. J., and Danko, W. D. *The Millionaire Next Door: The Surprising Secrets of America's Wealthy*. Atlanta: Longstreet Press, 1996.

Starcher, G. "Socially Responsible Enterprise Restructuring." [http://www.ebbf.org/sper.html], 2000.

Taylor, B., Chait, R., and Holland, T. "The New Work of the Nonprofit Board." *Harvard Business Review*, Sept. 1, 1996.

U.S. Census Bureau. "Geographical Mobility: March 1998 to March 1999 (Update)." *March 1991 Current Population Survey*. Washington, D.C.: U.S. Government Printing Office, 1999.

*Working Smart* (Growth Design Corporation newsletter). Fall, 1995.

Wright, A. P. "Too Closed for Comfort: Trustees Get a Grip on Excess Capacity." *Trustee*, Sept. 1997, 50(8), 22, 5p, 1c.

Zimmerman, D., and Skalko, J. *Reengineering Health Care: A Vision for the Future*. Franklin, Wis.: Eagle Press, 1994.

# Index

# Boards That Make a Difference

## A New Design for Leadership in Nonprofit and Public Organizations, Second Edition

*John Carver*

J ohn Carver's groundbreaking Policy Governance model has influenced the way public and nonprofit boards operate around the world. Now, as widespread experience with the model accumulates, Carver enriches his definitive exposition with updated policy samples, a new chapter on the process of policy development, and additional resources for various types of boards. Carver debunks the entrenched beliefs about board roles and functions that hamper dedicated board members. With creative insight and commonsense practicality, he presents a bold new approach to board job design, board-staff relationships, the chief executive role, performance monitoring, and virtually every aspect of the board-management relationship. In their stead, he offers a board model designed to produce policies that make a difference, missions that are clearly articulated, standards that are ethical and prudent, meetings, officers, and committees that work, and leadership that supports the fulfillment of long-term goals.

"This book should be in the library of everyone who serves—or aspires to serve—on the governing board of any organization, large or small, nonprofit or corporate. Better than any other available resource, it tells what the roles of board members are and what they must and shouldn't do. An indispensable guidebook to leadership excellence."
—George Weber, secretary general, *International Federation of Red Cross and Red Crescent Societies, Geneva*

"John Carver's book is important reading for chief executives and directors alike. This book's sound premises regarding proper role delineation and its practical advice about how to affect due diligence combine to provide an invaluable resource to any board dedicated to efficiency and high-quality performance."
—John R. Seffrin, CEO, *American Cancer Society*

| Hardcover | 272 pages | ISBN 0-7879-0811-8 | $32.00 |

Price subject to change without notice.